James Penny Boyd

Recent Indian Wars, under the Lead of Sitting Bull, and Other Chiefs

With a Full Account of the Messiah Craze, and Ghost Dances

James Penny Boyd

Recent Indian Wars, under the Lead of Sitting Bull, and Other Chiefs
With a Full Account of the Messiah Craze, and Ghost Dances

ISBN/EAN: 9783337010256

Printed in Europe, USA, Canada, Australia, Japan

Cover: Foto ©ninafisch / pixelio.de

More available books at **www.hansebooks.com**

SITTING BULL.

RECENT INDIAN WARS,

UNDER THE LEAD OF

SITTING BULL,

AND OTHER CHIEFS;

WITH A FULL ACCOUNT OF

The ✸ Messiah ✸ Craze,

AND

Ghost ✸ Dances.

By JAMES P. BOYD, A. M.,

Author of "Life of General Grant," "Political History of U. S." Etc.

PUBLISHERS UNION.

1891.

WHITE EAGLE.

CONTENTS.

	Page.
Introductory,	3

CHAPTER I.
The War with the Pueblos, ... 15

CHAPTER II.
The Shoshone Uprising, ... , . 26

CHAPTER III.
Wars with the California Tribes, ... 34

CHAPTER IV.
A Yuma Massacre, ... 39

CHAPTER V.
The Rogue River Wars, ... 49

CHAPTER VI.
War with the Cheyennes, ... 58

CHAPTER VII.
Navajo Hostilities, ... 63

CHAPTER VIII.
The Affair of Mountain Meadow, ... 73

CHAPTER IX.
The Spokane Wars, ... 79

CONTENTS.

CHAPTER X.
	Page.
The Fierce Apaches and Arrapahoes,	85

CHAPTER XI.
Wars with the Ogallallas and Crows,	99

CHAPTER XII.
The Piegan Punishment,	110

CHAPTER XIII.
Modoc and Lava Bed,	117

CHAPTER XIV.
Custer and the Sioux,	129

CHAPTER XV.
The Nez Perces Wars,	153

CHAPTER XVI.
The Utes of White River,	165

CHAPTER XVII.
The Messiah Craze and Ghost Dance,	175

CHAPTER XVIII.
Mastering the Situation,	211

CHAPTER XIX.
Sentiment Respecting the Uprising,	288

List of Illustrations.

	Page.
Sitting Bull,	Frontispiece.
White Eagle,	3
White Thunder,	6
Big Joseph,	11
John Grass,	14
Ration Day at an Agency,	16
Red Cloud,	131
Standing Holly, (Sitting Bull's Daughter),	134
Sioux on the Warpath,	139
A Group of Sioux Chiefs,	142
General Nelson A. Miles,	179
Ghost Dance,	182
Front of the Company Street, 1st U. S. Cavalry at Ft. Keogh,	187
Tepees of Sioux Chiefs at Ft. Thunder,	190

LIST OF ILLUSTRATIONS.

	Page
Bear-Comes-Back-Again,	196
View of the Bad Lands,	205
Sitting Bull (late photograph),	211
Officers of 20th and 25th Infantry, at Ft. Keogh,	214
A Hostile Encampment,	219
Interior of Cavalry Tent, at Pine Ridge,	222

WHITE THUNDER.

Introductory.

THE recent uprising of the Sioux Indians and their kindred tribes in the Dakotas, added to the possibility of a great conspiracy among all the mountain tribes of the West, for the purpose of rapine, at a date not later than the spring and summer of 1891, has excited lively interest in all that appertains to the Red Race, especially their wars, numbers, and the method of dealing with them.

The policy of the National Government toward the Indian, prior to his removal beyond the Mississippi, was the cruel policy of extinction. Indians were then more numerous than now, braver, more in the way. It cost a great deal to subdue them, more to extinguish them. They were seldom friendly, but often dangerous enemies, prone to ally themselves with foreign nations, as was natural, for every civilized nation has treated them better than our own.

The time came, but not until the Indian had fully proved that he preferred extinction to slavery or to the adoption of our civilization, when it was deemed a wise policy to rid the lands east of the

Mississippi of his presence. All west of the Mississippi was then deemed sufficiently open to make it safe for the transfer to take place. But in practice it did not prove so. The eastern Indian had a little of the salt of commerce in him and had cultivated some of the ways of industry. He found himself among enemies of his own race. He was scarcely less in the way—an Indian is always in the way—of our own advance. So, as one of its first acts of mercy, the Government availed itself of the cheap lands at its disposal, and fell to the policy of a species of Indian colonization, which took the form of granting the migrating tribes large reservations and a sort of self-government, provided they would stay at home, behave themselves and do whatever was asked of them. Most of the tribes did this, and those who confined themselves to the Indian Territory, have had little occasion to regret the disposition which was made of them.

But that did not settle the Indian question by any means. The trans-Mississippi lands, the lands of sterile plains, lofty plateaus and mountain gorges, were peopled by numerous tribes, more nomadic by reason of their immense territorial spaces, than those of the east; dependent for food on a lesser variety but a larger size of game, as the buffalo, and actuated by a savagery

INTRODUCTORY.

quite as cunning and remorseless as any we read of in the history of colonial times. While many of these tribes are of the same general family, as indicated by their speech and habits, the larger ones are quite distinct, being separated by wide plains or high mountain barriers. All of them have ever evinced the traditional hostility to the white man, regarding his advance as dispossession and his methods of life as obnoxious.

Therefore, the West-Mississippi tribes soon came into a prominence which even overshadowed that which the East-Mississippi tribes had occupied in history. The constant opening of new lands by the whites, the discovery of gold in California, the development of agriculture and mining in various directions, all of the forces of our civilization which constantly brought the white man into contact with the western natives, just as constantly produced clashes of the two races. The consequences have been that pioneering has always been fraught with its old time dangers, and that the white man has been compelled to literally fight his way to the Pacific.

For fifty years the Government has tried to shape a policy for the western Indian, which had some of the elements of intelligent humanity in it, but all of those years have been characterized by violent Indian outbreaks, and often protracted and bloody wars. All recognize that the policy of force which the pioneer uses when left to himself, is based only on his selfishness, and is essentially brutal. That the Government might escape the appearance of sanctioning perpetual murders, and the expense of continual embroilment, by sending troops whenever called for to protect settlers who had become involved with the Indians, it adopted, as most expedient, a policy for the Western Indians similar to that it had tried on with the Eastern. While it did not ask them to migrate, as it had done with the Eastern Indians, and for the reason that it could not force them, it allotted to them the lands which had constituted their hunting grounds and called them "reservations." To these reservations it gave crude metes and bounds, and within their limits the respective tribes were to dwell. To those tribes who had thus materially curtailed their hunting grounds by giving up large and valuable areas, the Government offered a consideration, sometimes very handsome, and the increment of this consideration, or, so to speak, the interest on it, was to go to the support of the tribe in the shape of annual supplies. In other instances, where the possibility of living by the chase within the reservation had been entirely cut off, the consideration was a set of

BIG JOSEPH.

supplies, equal to a living, to be distributed periodically at regularly established agencies and through authorized Government agents.

The scheme looked plausible. It had a show of fairness about it, from the white man's standpoint. It was charitable in the respect that the Indian need not necessarily starve under it. It would segregate the tribes and thus diminish the possibility of conspiracies and alliances to carry on extensive wars. It would set free immense tracts of land for the progressive white man. It would encourage the Indian to try agriculture and the peaceful arts on his own hook. Even if he had to be fed outright and in full by the Government, it would be cheaper in the end, than the annual expenditure of millions to maintain an army with which to fight him. Thus segregated, and his territory defined, missionary enterprise would become possible in his midst.

The difficulties in the way have been that only the weaker and tamer tribes have accepted the policy. The larger and wilder tribes have not proven amenable. Their example has always proven a source of dissatisfaction with those upon the reservations. Again, the Indian, naturally suspicious and discontented, has not found that faith on the part of the Government and his white surroundings, he was given to expect. Granted that he is a mal-odorous and savage being, still he has rights. It is doubtful whether the number of Indian wars and massacres has been diminished by a single one, by the adoption of the reservation and agency policy. Certainly, all the late Indian outbreaks have involved a complaint on the part of the tribes that the Government had violated its solemn compacts with them. Some of these wars have been fierce and protracted and have cost many precious lives and vast sums of money.

It is our purpose to describe these Indian wars of modern times. In themselves they make a thrilling story and are worthy of reading on that account alone. But they are even more valuable at this time, as showing how the western Indian and western pioneering repeat the older history of adventure, of daring, of cunning, of massacre, and how illy prepared our civilization is, even after an acquaintance of two hundred years, to evolve an Indian policy which is at all creditable to our intelligence, humanity and Christianity. It may be that a study of the Indian wars for the last fifty years will show wherein our policy has been weak, and, mayhap, it may show what ought to be done to remove the badge of shame from our management of one of the most vital questions which now confronts us as a nation. Just now, General Miles proposes to transfer the entire control of the Indian question from the civil to the military department of the Government, his theory being that force goes further with an Indian than suasion. If the step would insure a greater degree of fairness in dealing with him, Heaven help the nation to take it.

That this little book may delight all, and at the same time help us to solve one of the knottiest problems of the day, is the sincere wish of its author.

JOHN GRASS.

Chapter I.
WAR WITH THE PUEBLOS.

IN June, 1846, the advance of the then "Army of the West," under Colonel Kearney, marched from Fort Leavenworth into New Mexico. It was met at Fort Bent by two troops of cavalry. In the following autumn a regiment of men under Colonel Price started for the scene, together with a Mormon detatchment of five hundred men. Altogether, the gathering at Fort Bent consisted of nearly seventeen hundred men, six companies of which were cavalry, and two batteries of artillery.

The object was to expel the Mexicans and Indians from New Mexico. When the American army crossed the plains and learned that it was to be confronted at Apache Canon—the natural approach to Santa Fe—by 5,000 Mexicans, it naturally concluded that a desperate battle was at hand. But, strange to say, their advance was unimpeded, for the Mexicans, on learning of the approach of the Americans beat a hasty retreat. The conquest of New Mexico thus far, was easy and bloodless. The Mexican army was disbanded at Santa Fe, and the northern invaders entered this oldest city in the United States in peace.

Having accomplished its mission, for the most part, this little army of 1,700 men, divided up for the purpose of conquering further empires. Kearney started with 300 men for California, and Colonel Doniphan marched with 850 men for the conquest of Chihuahua. The result of this last expedition was a battle at Bracito, with an army of 1,200 Mexicans, in which the latter were completely routed.

Before Kearney left for the west, he organized a provisional government for the Territory with Charles Bent as Governor. He was the builder and occupant of Bent's fort on the Arkansas. It was a strong fort, and Bent was a man of great courage and large experience with the rough and ready ways of the frontier. There were, as yet, but few Americans in his jurisdiction. The people were mostly Mexicans, Pueblo Indians and wild Indians. The wild Indians had been friendly to the Americans, because the Mexicans were in control, but now that the Americans were in control, they had, according to Indian nature become hostile. The Mexicans, who remained were of very little account, except as disturbers of the peace, for they were of that class which had done service as peons for the grandees who had fled.

RATION DAY AT AN AGENCY.

The Pueblo Indians were the most numerous, intelligent and reliable of the three. They embraced a number of tribes, of very ancient origin, akin to each other in speech and habit, far advanced in intelligence, somewhat Christianized by the Catholic church, given to agriculture and art, and resident for the most part in permanent towns—whence their name, Pueblo.

At the time of our conquest of New Mexico, they inhabited some twenty-six towns, some of which were in Arizona, occupied by the Moquis, or "death" portion, and by the Zuni portion, also in Arizona, the remaining portions being in the Rio Grande Valley. In all respects they are a most interesting people, having a history, running back in accurate chapters to the Spanish Conquest, and traditions that connect them with the ancient Aztec races of the Pacific slope. That they had been a high grade people, is shown by the remains of art in their country. Some of the most remarkable ruins of pottery ovens, house architecture and irrigating appliances in the country, one found in their midst. The outlines of many ancient towns are yet distinct, and it is clear that they possessed the art of both weaving and writing.

Notwithstanding the fact that the Pueblos ranked as an honest, brave, sober, intelligent and industrious people, to whose forefathers we are willing to attribute a high civilization and the origin of the hyeroglyphics, the cave dwellings, the many wonderful ruins of art and architecture found in the valleys and canons from the Rio Grande to the Mohave Desert, they were nevertheless true to their Indian origin in the respect that as soon as the American troops left Santa Fe for other points they began to conspire to take advantage of a weakened situation. They found ample encouragement in the disappointed Mexican leaders who added recklessness to their discomfiture. An uprising was planned for December of the year 1846, and its object was to murder or dispel every American and friendly Indian found in the newly created department. The signals for the uprising had been agreed upon and were ready, but as fortune would have it, the plot was revealed three days in advance of the time set. Many of the ringleaders were arrested, and there was a general stampede of the rest to Mexico. Governor Bent issued a pacifying proclamation, which tided over the excitement, but insurrection smoldered for only a time. In January 1847, the Pueblos rose in a body and demanded the release of certain of their number retained as prisoners. Their demand was unheeded, whereupon they made an attack and killed the sheriff and his assistants. Their success met with encouragement at the hands of several of the original conspirators, and they invested the home of Governor Bent. His wife warned him of his danger. Seeing the futility of contending with so numerous and bloodthirsty a host, he called for assistance from the neighbors who were mostly Mexicans. They refused him aid and almost mockingly told him that he might as well make up his mind to die. Meanwhile he had received two wounds from the arrows of the Pueblos. Retreating to his room, his wife brought him his pistols and asked him to avenge himself, even if he must die. He declined to use them saying, "I will kill no one of them, for your sake and for that of my children. My death is all these infatuated and cruel people ask at present."

The savages had already torn the roof off the house and began pouring into his room. He appealed to their manhood and honor, but in vain. "Every American in New Mexico should die!" they exclaimed, "and you shall go with them." An arrow followed their bloody resolve, then another and another, but the method was not swift enough. A bullet sped through his heart and as he fell, a chief, stepping forward, snatched one of his pistols and shot him in the face. Then they took his scalp, and stretching it on a board with brass nails, carried it through the streets in triumph. After this, the Indians running wild with excitement, carried their massacre into every house whose occupant was an American. All of the leading officials perished or made their escape with difficulty. Whole families were exterminated. The priests, who were partly blamed for inciting the insurrection had to intercede to stay its cruelty.

Word of the insurrection spread among the Indian tribes and the uprising became general. Word also was carried to Sante Fe, and the Americans rallied for resistance. Traveling parties were captured and shot by the Indians, settlements were attacked and broken up; guards were driven away from the cattle ranches and the cattle were stampeded and driven off. At length the hostiles surrounded the strong corral at Turley's mill. The owner was a conspicuous man in the Territory, and stood well with the Indians. He had a strong band of help about him, who on the approach of the Indians hastened within the corral and prepared for defence. The Indians closed in upon the place and offered to spare Turley's life, but said they had killed the Governor at Fernandez, and that every American in the Territory must die. Turley defied them.

The Indians then began the attack under cover of the rocks and bushes. The defenders made a loop hole of every window in the mill and laid many an Indian low with their bullets. All day the siege was maintained, and at nightfall firing ceased, but the hostiles crept closer under cover of darkness. They originally numbered 500, and now their strength was being increased by new accessions. In the morning hostilities began again, and with increased determination on the part of the Indians. They got a foothold within the corral, where scores of them, including one of their most popular chiefs, fell victims to the bullets of the defenders. Baffled o'er and o'er again by the bravery of the besieged, the Indians renewed every attack more desperately, only to find their numbers reduced by the unerring aim of the defenders. Finally the Indians got close enough to fire the mill. The flames were extinguished only to break out again. Ammunition was running low. The defenders gave up hope, but resolved to hold on until night, and then try to escape, each one striking out for himself. This they did, but in the effort to pierce the cordon about them all fell victims except two, who managed to reach Santa Fe as bearers of the horrid news.

On their arrival Col. Price started immediately with his command of 350 infantry and four howitzers for the scene. His force was augmented by a company of volunteers, who comprised the indignant citizens of Sante Fe. They hastened to Taos, where they met the hostiles under the lead of a Mexican officer, and battle was at once joined. It was but a brief fight for the enemy was quickly dislodged from its strong hold by the howitzers, and then thrown into confused retreat by a splendid charge on the part of the Americans. They left 32 dead on the field together with the usual compliment of wounded.

Col. Price now received reinforcements, and with an army of 500 pushed on to the canon of Embudo, where the enemy were posted in force. They were in a strong position, but were charged upon and driven out with considerable loss. Thence they retreated up the valley to a strong pueblo, and there was nothing to do for the American army but to follow. The pursuit involved great hardship, for a deep snow had fallen and many officers and soldiers perished by being frozen, or through colds contracted by sleeping without tents or blankets. At the pueblo they found the enemy strongly fortified. The village was surrounded by thick adobe walls, at whose corners rose high bulwarks capable of sheltering 800 men. Every point of the wall was pierced for rifles, and every point without was flanked by projecting angles.

It would not do to rush indiscriminately upon such a stronghold. The army was carefully deployed, and positions were chosen for the artillery. For two hours the batteries played on a corner of the fortification, but without effect. Then there was a wait over night for further ammunition. During this time a plan of attack was matured. The village was surrounded on three sides; on the east and west by troops, on the north by the artillery. The artillery was to play till it made a breach in the walls, but it proved ineffective for this purpose. The troops on the other sides were then commanded to close and charge. They scaled the walls by means of ladders, fired the roofs of the buildings, cut holes through walls, threw in lighted shells and fought desperately for the vantage. Meanwhile, the artillery was busy landing shot and shell into the inclosure and distracting the attention of the enemy. Venturesome as was the attack of the Americans, they found no such resistance as they anticipated, for the enemy was never given a moment to concentrate its fire. It was driven by slow degrees into the church building in a corner of the pueblo, where it made its last desperate stand. A breach had been made in the outer walls through which a cannon was run. This was turned on the church and in ten rounds the walls began to crumble. Pioneers were formed who rushed into the church with axes and began to batter down the doors. The Indians broke and fled to other portions of the pueblo. Those who tried to escape to the mountains were shot down by the troops stationed without, those who gained cover within the pueblo were searched out and given no quarter. Chiefs fell who wore the clothing of white men killed at Turley's mill. One was slain who was dressed in the coat of Governor Bent. Altogether 150 of the insurgents were slain and twice that many wounded out of a total of 650. On the morning after the battle a delegation of men and women came to Colonel Price bearing crucifixes and images, and begged mercy on their knees. It was granted on condition that the ringleaders should be surrendered for trial under the law.

The conditions were accepted, and the culprits were taken into custody by the army. Many of them were Mexican desperadoes, who had incited the Indians to rebellion. Scores of them were tried and convicted. Fourteen of them were executed and the rest were pardoned on condition of future good behavior. The victory of our army was complete. On no occasion since have the Pueblos turned against the United States Government. Their chastisement was sufficient for all time. Since then they have departed from the Mexican traditions and remitted much of their savagery. Most of them have drifted into citizenship, and have yielded to missionary enterprise. In 1874 the Government had its last difficulty with them, which was largely a religious affair, and was peaceably adjusted.

Chapter II.

THE SHOSHONE UPRISING.

THE great Shoshone stock of Indians originally embraced the most powerful tribes of the extreme Northwest, grouped into families according to the topography of the country. The Modocs, Bannocks, Snakes, Utes, Kiowas and Comanches are of Shoshone origin. Akin to them also were the three families of tribes which extend from the Blue Mountains of Oregon to the Canadian border. The northernmost of these families is the Selish, to which belong the Flatheads and Coeur D' Alenes. South of them is the Saptin family, embracing the Nez Perces, Walla-Wallas, Klickitats, Yakimas and Pelouse. Below the Columbia River are the Wailatpu, Cayuses and Moleles. The Spokanes are found on the Spokane branch of Clark's Fork.

In early days, the emigrant road through the Grand Ronde, over the Blue Mountains and down the Walla-Walla to the Columbia, opened up what was regarded as a fine field for missionary enterprise, and a large and prosperous mission station was started at Wailatpu, for the purpose of civilizing and christianizing the Wailatpus and Cayuses. Another mission of similar proportions sprang up on the Lapwai, at its junction with the Clear Water, which was a centre of evangelical influence with the Nez Perces. Still another came into being near the Spokane River, far to the north. Down the Columbia, at the Dalles, and again in the Williamette, were other missions, mostly under Methodist auspices.

The climate and soil were inviting. Missionary work went bravely on among tribes, which seemed kindly disposed and amenable. The missions became quite independent little settlements, with mills, shops, schools, churches, farms and a sufficient number of people to constitute a society. But there was one misfortune attending settlement and missionary enterprise in this region. The old and powerful Hudson Bay Company had a fortified trading post at Wallula, the mouth of the Walla-Walla. The headquarters of said company was further down, at Fort Vancouver. The officers of this company had favored missionary enterprise from the States, and the presence of its strong and well fortified trading ports was regarded as a means of safety for the remote missionary stations.

This Company, however, came to represent England in her designs upon our Northern frontier. Those designs were to push the Canadian borders down so as to embrace a control of the Columbia River. The company officials made overtures to the missionaries and settlers, which had to be rejected on both moral and patriotic grounds. These officials then began to antagonize settlement and to corrupt the natives. They sold the Indians rum, guns and ammunition, on the plea that it made their hunting more successful. They opposed agriculture, lest it diminish the Company's food supply. When it became manifest that the Americans were up to their game, and were forcing a settlement of the country, the Company fought every step of northward progress. It opposed cattle company and saw mill, with rivals, and at last went so far as to warn intruders from lands it claimed by virtue of no title at all. Emigrant trains were blockaded at Fort Hall, and several trains were forced to deflect southward into California. Probably the worst feature of the Company's opposition was that it acted as convoy to the Jesuit Priests who were bitter against the Protestant missionaries from the south.

The jealousy and bitterness which sprang up between the Catholic and Protestant missions passed to the Indians in intensified form. They became restless and turbulent, fit subjects for crime, should a pretext offer. The Jesuits had decidedly the most influence over the Indians. Their missions were encouraged and protected by the powerful Company at their back. They could use its employes as heralds and interpreters. They were in stronger force than the Protestants. In 1847, a newly appointed Jesuit Bishop of Oregon came to Walla-Walla and held a conference with Ta-wai-tu, a Catholic Cayuse chief. It was given out that the object of the conference was to devise means for dispossessing the Protestants and occupying the sites of their missions. At any rate, the Bishop took up permanent quarters at Minatilla, in a house offered by Ta-wai-tu, twenty-five miles south of Wailatpu, and in the rear of the flourishing mission there. This was on November 27, 1847. On November 29, while the mill at Wailatpu was running, the school in session, all the artisans at their trades, and the missionaries moving about in their errands of mercy, several Indians appeared upon the scene, headed by Tamsaky, who suddenly drew a tomahawk from beneath his blanket and brained the venerable Dr. Whitman, the head of the mission.

In an instant all was confusion within the mission grounds. The striking down of Dr. Whitman was the signal for a general attack by the Indians, who now appeared in all parts of the grounds—at the mill, the shops, the chapel and the schools. The Indians were well armed with knives, tomahawks, pistols and Hudson Bay Company muskets. The miller fell at his post, bravely fighting. The tailor and carpenter went down at their benches. The teacher made a brave stand at the schoolroom, but was soon numbered among the victims. The frightened children fled to the loft for hiding, but were soon brought down and driven into a huddled mass by a cordon of savages who held them trembling prisoners by threats of shooting. The women who had fled for safety to the central mansion and had taken refuge in the upper stories, were ordered down in order that the house might be fired. The fate of most of them was more horrible than if they had submitted to being burned. Mrs. Whitman and others were foully murdered. Many were taken prisoners and carried away into bondage. A few managed to escape slaughter and captivity for the time being and remained in hiding in the houses.

Night came on and the Indians withdrew to their lodges, after finishing their plundering. It was a night of terror for the few survivors at the mission. Under cover of the darkness, one man escaped and made his way to Lapwai. The Osborne family escaped and reached Walla-Walla. Several fugitives were caught the next day and murdered. The young girls, daughters of teachers and mechanics, were distributed among the braves who had been instrumental in the murder of their parents. The destruction of the mission was complete. The murder of its numerous occupants had been brought about in the most effective way, showing clearly the existence of a well matured plot on the part of the Indians and their advisers.

When word of the uprising and massacre reached Oregon City, the Governor ordered a levy of troops and in twenty-four hours a company of forty-two men were on their way to the Dalles, where fugitives from all the missions above were coming. Here the troops remained for the purpose of guarding the passage of fugitives and restored captives to safe places below, while awaiting re-inforcements, till February 1848. Being re-inforced, Captain Lee sent a scouting party against the Des Chutes, the nearest of the hostiles, which defeated them in a battle on February 28. The main body of 160 troops moved toward Wailatpu, near which they met a strong body of Indians. A desperate battle was fought in which the Indians lost 20 warriors and 40 horses, together with all their goods.

As the troops proceeded, the French Canadian leader, Finlay, who managed the massacre at Wailatpu, attempted to entrap them by a pretence of peace. He had about 500 Indians at his disposal, and the Americans could only advance by keeping close in line. They literally fought their way to Wailatpu, where they established a fort and called on the adjoining tribes to come in for a talk. The Nez Perces and most of the Cayuses came and were prompt to disavow participation in the massacre. Chief Joseph, of the Nez Perces, promised to deliver up all the murderers found in his tribe. Those who remained hostile in the neighboring tribes were pursued by the troops and defeated in repeated battles. They were finally driven into the neighboring mountains and back into the Nez Perces country, with the loss of many of their warriors and most of their cattle. The troops remained at the various forts they had established during the year 1848, and the tribes of the murderers were forced to pursue a wandering life in the mountain gorges, not daring to return to their homes. This state of affairs continued during 1849 and 1850. In the latter year they purchased peace by surrendering five of the murderous chiefs, who were tried and hung.

All the mission houses at Wailatpu were burned by the Indians, and to-day mounds of earth mark their site. On the hillside is the common grave of the victims. The position of the garden is marked by a few fruit trees and clusters of the flowers planted by those who passed away, ere civilization could give them its guarantees of peace and safety.

CHAPTER III.

WARS WITH THE CALIFORNIA TRIBES.

WHILE the Oregon volunteers were still at the Dalles in defence of their homes, gold was discovered in paying quantities at Mormon Island and in Sutter's mill race in California. In a trice all California was mad, and the gold craze spread all over the United States. A flood of emigration by land and sea poured into the gold coasts of the Pacific. The year 1849 became historic and the forty-niner a character in the tragedy and comedy of the times.

The flood of emigration, the crush of enterprise, the selfishness of greed, the cruelty of acquisition, under the circumstances, proved to be greater evils for the Indians than even the discovery of Columbus and the Spanish occupation. Gold miners had no patience with Indians. They would ransack the mountains in search of claims. They would kill all who interfered with their supposed rights. The Indian knew this, and as a rule "vacated the ranche" on a single warning. If he stood for his rights, the policy of the Government was to get rid of him as quickly as possible by buying him out, so as to avoid bloodshed.

Generally speaking the Indians of California were not fighters. The Yrekas in the north were brave and gave much trouble, but the tribes to the south lacked union and spirit. The entire Indian population did not exceed 30,000, of whom not over half were classed as wild Indians. The first clash with the California Indians came at Mormon Island, and it was instigated by miners, who perhaps sought an occasion to teach their hostile neighbors what they might expect if they did not clear the way for exploration and occupancy. It was a cruel " set-to" which resulted fatally to a number on both sides, but which resulted in impressing the Indians with the conviction that the vicinity of a gold mining camp, was the least desirable place in the world for their own camps.

As miners pushed their way into the mountains and mining camps became thick in the gulches and valleys, the difficulties with the Indians increased. Skirmishes became frequent, but as a rule the Indians were marauders and cattle thieves, rather than open, organized warriors. They were "pestiferous," as the mining phrase went, and in this respect were more objects of malice than if they had been regularly on the warpath. The Government hearkened to the calls for aid to put them down. It could not send troops so far, but it sent 100,000 arms. The miners quickly formed a local militia and would, no doubt, have made a war of extermination upon the Indians of the Territory, had not the Government in a spirit of humanity, hit on the plan of treating with them and giving them a place on reservations. Most of the tribes took their places gladly on reservations, but some of the mountain tribes either feared to come in or preferred the freedom of their mountain fastnesses.

These were treated as hostiles, and the improvised militia of California quickly made war upon them. The California wars of 1851-52 were chiefly those brought about by efforts to catch these hostiles and corral them on reservations. The hostiles of the San Joaquin Valley were hunted down and brought to terms by the celebrated Mariposa Battalion. Jose Rey, chief of the Chowchillas, was defeated in several engagements and finally lost his life in a battle which determined the fate of his tribe. The Yosemites, or "Grizzly Bears," who lived in the wonderful canon valley which perpetuates their name, were brave warriors by repute, but when confronted by the militia they offered little resistance. The wars in and around Sacramento Valley amounted to but little more than a succession of skirmishes. By 1853 the California tribes were pretty generally subdued and driven on to the five reservations set apart for them. These reservations were badly managed by the Government agents, who drew plentiful supplies from the Government but gave the Indians none. The consequence was the reservations fell into disrepute and were practically abandoned. White settlers took mean advantage of the absence of the Indians, the latter having been forced into a nomadic life and having become more thievish and cowardly than ever before. Every Indian theft, every attempt on their part to scout and live, or to come back on their reservations to assert their rights, became a cause for war upon them, and it is quite probable that more perished in the difficulties which thus arose, than in all the prior efforts to conquer them. Over 150 Indians were massacred by the white settlers at Nome Cult in 1858, the only excuse being that they had driven off the cattle of the settlers from the reservation, because they were consuming the acorns on which the Indians depended for food. At King's River the Indians were shot down by scores, and driven away because the Government would not support them and they had be come a nuisance. In these humanitarian efforts to exterminate the natives, the settlers had the support of the State militia and there was no sentiment against this kind of murder. At Mattole Station and Humboldt Bay, similar massacres took place and there was no mercy shown to a refractory Indian. The next morning after the massacre at Humboldt Bay, sixty corpses of Indian men, women, boys and girls, showed how impious had been their refusal to go off to the then secluded region of Mendocino.

The character of the California settlers, gathered from all the ends of the earth, inspired by greed, with a golden stake in hand, was such as to make the Indian wars of California frequent, short and decisive. They were wars which involved excessive cruelty, wars of extermination. The miners were a society by themselves, and a unit in their own protection. There was, of course, a powerful necessity for protection, as was shown not only in their wars with Indians, but in those stern measures which became the code of justice of their "Vigilance Committees." They were really at war with themselves, and peace and the reign of law came only after the rope had taught many of their own number, the same lessons their shotguns had impressed on the Indians.

Chapter IV.

A YUMA MASSACRE.

THE Indian tribes of Arizona and the line of the Colorado River, have ever been an interesting study. Two large nations, of which the Yuma is one, were agricultural and peaceful. They came early under the influence of the Spanish, and proved useful as a bulwark against the fierce and powerful Apaches. But there were blendings of these tribes with the bolder and wilder Apaches, with the result that many degraded tribes arose, which possessed the virtues of neither, but for whose actions one or the other of the leading tribes had to be responsible. Thus a dangerous and freebooting tribe, called Tontos, was allied by birth to both the Yumas and Apaches, and if they committed an outrage, it was either a Yuma or Apache outrage, according to the interest either had in it, or the apology offered for it.

As a rule these tribes, excepting the dreaded Apaches, succumbed to the authority of the United States, after the Mexican Conquest and the Gadsden purchase, without open war. So that while there are no startling records of hostilities in their midst, there are several thrilling accounts of massacres. The one which led to the complete subjugation of the Arizona tribes, always excepting the Apaches, is a sample of many. In 1850 a party composed of eighty emigrants, men, women and children, started for Arizona, intending to locate within the protective range of Ft. Yuma, then a military camp at the junction of the Gila with the Colorado.

By the time this party reached the junction of the north and south roads near Santa Fe, they became so divided by religious dissensions that they split; one faction taking the northern, the other the southern route. By the close of the year the southern party reached Tucson, where they were gladly received by the Mexican citizens, who were greatly alarmed at the excesses of the Apaches. A part of the party agreed to settle there temporarily. The rest, embracing three families, the largest of which was the Oatman family, started on across the "ninety mile desert." After many escapes from roving Apache bands they reached the country of the Pimas, where they found rest. The Pimas had, however, but little food for strangers, and the Oatman family, in a spirit of desperation started alone for Ft. Yuma. After crossing the desert of Gila Bend and striking the Gila, the roads became almost impassable.

On a certain day, while struggling with their difficult situation, unloading their wagon at the foot of steep hills and carrying their goods upon their shoulders, so that their starved oxen might be able to take the empty wagon up, they saw evidences of Indians about them. The next day as they broke camp, at the head of a little valley of the Gila which is to this day known as Oatman Flat, they were suddenly surrounded by a troop of Tonto Indians armed with bows and arrows and clubs. Knowing that a show of fear would be fatal, Oatman assured his family and coolly asked the miscreants to sit down for a talk. He passed pipes and tobacco, and each one took a whiff of amity. The Oatman family, meanwhile, kept up their preparations for the onward march as if unconcerned about results. This gave the Indians opportunity to gauge the strength of the party. They asked for food. Oatman told them he had barely enough to sustain his family till it reached Ft. Yuma. They did not accept his excuse, but grew clamorous and angry. In order to appease them Oatman divided his little store with them. They demanded more, which Oatman refused, not wishing to rob his family entirely.

The Indians drew off, held a hurried consultation, scanned the horizon to see that no help was near, and then with wild yells rushed upon the helpless family with their merciless clubs. Oatman was beaten to the ground and his skull crushed by repeated blows of the clubs. His son, Lorenzo, a boy of twelve years, received repeated blows which rendered him insensible. Mrs. Oatman leaped from the wagon and clasped her youngest child, a boy of two years, to her bosom. The savages dashed upon her and beat out the life of mother and child together. The daughter Lucy was beaten into a shapeless mass and left an unrecognizable corpse on the bloody soil. Another daughter of four years, was similarly dispatched. A brother of six years, was the next to fall. Two daughters, Olive and Mary, were spared to become captives. After the massacre was complete, the camp was plundered. Seeing signs of life in the prostrate Lorenzo, the miscreants stripped him of his clothing and threw his body down over a pile of rugged rocks. It rolled helpless on to platform at the base, full twenty feet below, where it lay through the following night and until the next day. Then consciousness slowly returned.

He opened his eyes to find the sun shining full in his face. He wiped the clotted blood from his face, felt that his scalp had been torn off, straightened his crooked and stiffened limbs, and gazed about him to find out where he was. The bloodstained rocks over which he had been thrown told him how he had come there, and soon the terrible memory of the day before rushed in on his dazed brain. After a painful struggle, he gained his feet, and under a frenzied impulse crawled up the rocks to the scene of the massacre. The broken wagon, the remnants of goods strewn around, the ghastly faces of murdered parents, brothers and sisters, proved to be too much for him. He sank in a faint, and when he recovered his only thought was to escape a repetition of the dreadful sight. He dragged his pain racked form down toward the Gila, drank of its muddy waters, bathed his bruised body therein, and then crawled away to a cover, where he passed a day and night in sleep.

Finding himself able to walk with the aid of a stick, but being yet too delirious to judge of direction, he started he knew not whither. By mid-day he reached a pool of warm and muddy water, by the side of which he lay down and drank, only to fall asleep again in the sunshine. This rest gave him additional strength and he took up his journey, still ignorant of the direction but conscious that he was traversing a barren table-land. By nightfall he dropped in a faint from which he was aroused by the barking and growling of coyotes around him. Starting up with a yell and making such demonstration as he could with his stick, he drove the hungry beasts back and took up his slow and painful march. To his horror, he found they were following him. He drove them off with stones, but could not escape the horrid thought that he might drop down any moment through sheer exhaustion and thus become a prey to them.

The next day he found himself in the midst of a lonely cañon, and confronted by two Indians, who hastily drew their bows at sight of him. He raised his hand in surrender and spoke. They proved to be Pimas and friendly. When he told them of the massacre, they gave him some food and started for the scene, leaving him a blanket to sleep on and telling him to remain there till they came back. He did not know how long they would be gone, so after a refreshing sleep and a dread on awakening that they might prove treacherous, he clambored to the plain above and started on his unknown journey, taking rest and sleep wherever a guarded spot offered itself. One morning in looking across the plain he saw objects moving. They were rising an incline and when they appeared fully in view on top, he was rejoiced to find that they were wagons. He swooned through joy, and when he came to consciousness, the wagons of the two families left behind in Tucson were standing by him. He was refreshed with bread and milk, given clothing and his wounds were dressed. When he told his terrible story his friends retraced their steps to the Pimas, until they could be reinforced by other emigrants. These soon came, and then the reinforced party made its way to Fort Yuma, where Lorenzo was nursed back to health.

The Indian murderers made their way to the north of the Gila with their white captives, Olive and Mary Oatman. Their journey northward was one of great hardship. They were treated with savage cruelty and reduced to the condition of slaves. In 1851, a party of Mohaves visited the camp of the captors, and became the purchasers of the captives. Their condition was now much bettered, though they were still slaves. In a short while death came to Mary's relief, and Olive was left to bear her fate alone for a period of five years. In the midst of her despair at ever being rescued or making her escape, she was rejoiced one morning at finding a Yuma messenger from the Fort, in the midst of the tribe and with a demand for her release.

The rescue came about through Lorenzo. When he told his story at the fort, Colonel Heintzelman sent out several searching parties in vain. Soon after his forces were withdrawn, except a guard for the ferry. The Yumas drove this guard away and entered into a conspiracy to drive all Americans out of Arizona and Southern California. Colonel Heintzelman was returned with a larger force, and after a year of arduous and exciting work succeeded in reducing the Yumas to subjection and breaking up the conspiracy. Meanwhile Lorenzo had gone to California and drifted thence to Los Angeles. Here he learned that his sisters had been bought by the Mohaves, and he tried to interest the authorities in their rescue. This was in 1856. One man at Fort Yuma, the carpenter there, never lost his interest in the captives. He had as a bosom friend one Francisco, an Indian, who knew the terrorism inspired in his race by the show of power which Heintzelman's troopers had made. The carpenter and Francisco talked over the story of the captives as Lorenzo had learned, and Francisco agreed to rescue them, if the commander at the Fort would give him some goods as purchase money and agree to stand by him. This was brought about and Francisco started on his perilous mission. He held conference after conference with the chiefs, who stubbornly refused to surrender their captive, till Francisco made known to them that final refusal would bring upon them the full force of the United States troops, and that both Mohaves and Yumas would be wiped from the face of the earth.

They finally yielded to his arguments and Olive, after recovering from a faint occasioned by joy, was placed in charge of a delegation of the tribe which was authorized to deliver her in safety at the Fort, and receive the additional presents promised by Francisco. Her arrival was greeted by the troops with cheers and firing of cannon. Even the assembled Yumas, who had been trembling lest failure to make the rescue should bring on their heads the punishment threatened by Francisco, joined in the demonstrations of joy.

There was soon a more affecting meeting. Lorenzo was sent for to come to the Fort. Ten days of hard riding brought him to the embrace of his long lost sister. Tears streamed down the cheeks of the sturdy witnesses of a meeting which recalled the bloody separation of five years before, and the hardship and despair of every moment since. The two lived in California for some years and then went east. Francisco was made a chief by the Yumas, at the instigation of the whites. But he never secured their confidence, and could not prevent the Yuma and Mohave conspiracy, in 1857, against the Pimas and Maricopas, in which nearly all the Yuma warriors perished, Francisco himself being among them.

CHAPTER V.

THE ROGUE RIVER WARS.

WHEN Oregon was organized as a Territory in 1848, General Joe Lane was made Governor. Oregon was then an immense territory, embracing all the lands west of the Rocky Mountains, north of 42 degrees of latitude. Along its southern border were several tribes of hostile Indians—the Rogue Rivers, the Klamaths, the Modocs, the Shastas and Umpquas. None of these tribes had ever been friendly to the whites. The Umpquas had murdered eleven out of a trading party of fourteen men in 1834. A trading party of eight were attacked by the Rogue River Indians in 1835, and four of them killed. The Klamaths attacked Fremont's exploring expedition in 1845, and killed three of them before Kit Carson's skill could baffle the onslaught in a hand to hand conflict.

In 1851, the Rogue River Indians became so bold in their excursions, and these had become so frequent and deadly, that the Government was compelled to intervene. It sent Major Phil. Kearney to the scene, with a detachment of regulars. After manœuvreing for some time, he succeeded in bringing on an engagement in which he administered an unmerciful drubbing to the enemy. But this was not sufficient. They mustered new forces and courage, and stood for a second attack. This time Kearney resolved that the lesson of defeat should be effective. He got his men in good position, kept them well in hand and fought them so determinedly, that the enemy took to hasty flight toward the mountains, leaving a large number of their squaws and papooses in the hands of the victors. Governor Lane made the return of the captives the conditions of a peace which lasted for two years.

But the neighboring tribes were not so easily pacified. The Pitt River tribe massacred the engineers of a wagon road in 1852, and in the same year the Modocs attacked and shot down an emigrant party of thirty-three persons. This was the signal for open hostilities, and volunteer companies were organized and ordered to rendevous at Tule Lake. On the arrival of a California company a bloody battle took place, the Indians being on the lake in their canoes. They fought savagely but at a decided disadvantage, and were soon forced to retire out of range of the riflemen on the shore. The next day the victors discovered the remains of many murdered emigrants on the shores of the Lake.

Soon the California force was augmented by Oregon companies, and together they held the ground for many months, affording protection to emigrants and making occasional raids on the hostiles. However necessary this campaign may have been, its close brought no credit to the white soldiers. It is narrated that Captain Wright, who commanded the California forces, invited the Modoc warriors to a feast at which he tried to poison them. Finding his ruse a failure he turned the feast into a talk, amid which he grew angry and shot down two of his guests with his revolver. At this signal, his men rose up and fired their freshly loaded rifles into the assemblage, killing thirty-six outright. The remainder made their escape, but with such memory of treachery as that in future years, many times that number of white soldiers had to offer their lives in payment, and the Government had to forfeit millions of dollars for campaigning purposes.

On the return of Captain Wright to Yreka, he was welcomed by the citizens, but his vengeful visitation was not forgotten, for four years afterwards he was set upon by the Rogue Rivers at his agency and killed, together with 23 of his men. His bad faith bore its fruits with the entire Modoc people for years.

In California and Oregon, in those days the Government did not recognize the right of the Indian to treat for the sale of lands or for a reservation. The whites could squat where they pleased, do what they pleased, provoke war if they pleased and then call upon the troops for protection. As a rule the Oregon Indians were not unfriendly. The Whitman massacre was almost the only serious demonstration of hostility they had made. But when they saw their lands taken without compensation and their treaties nullified, they lost confidence and became more and more hostile. The Rogue Rivers became particularly irritable in 1853, and carried on almost constant war in their valley. General Lane was sent against them and fought a doubtful battle with a large force near Table Rock. He secured a treaty which lasted but a short while, for mutual murders soon became the rule, and massacre followed massacre in quick succession. It was evident, from the standpoint of the whites, that nothing but closely organized effort would suffice to teach the Indians the lesson they seemed to stand in need of. The Indians, on the other hand having a common grievance, and being actuated by a common dread of losing their lands altogether, through the encroachment of the whites, began to combine their strength. Leschi, a Nasqualla chief, preached a crusade against the whites, among all the tribes from the British borders to California, and infected them all with his hostility, except the Nez Perces.

The impatient tribes of the North opened the contest in 1855. The Yakimas murdered a party interested in coal mining on the Dwamish. The Indian agent at the Dalles was murdered by the same tribe. Two forces were sent against them, to be united in their country, but before they could unite, one of them was set upon, and driven back. The other was surrounded in a disadvantageous position, and only succeeded in escaping after great hardship. A stronger force of 350 regulars was organized and sent forward under Major Rains, but it could make no impression on the wily foe.

In the south, the whites were to blame for precipitating war by a cowardly attack on Old Sam's band of friendly Rogue Rivers, and the murder of several old men and helpless women and children. This foolish and cruel action inflamed the entire tribe, and as a consequence it began a campaign of indiscriminate burnings and murders, the most noted of which was the "Wagoner massacre." The troops, whether regulars or militia, retaliated in kind, and a warfare so indiscriminate and brutal as that which followed has never disgraced our annals. This was equally true in the south and in the north. The pervading policy on the part of the whites was Indian extermination, now and forever. The wars of 1855 shed no lustre on the arms of the whites. They only served to force the Indians into closer union and inspire them with a burning desire for revenge.

A change of policy came under General Wool who was made commander of the Department of the Pacific. He did not believe in the policy of extermination, nor in the employment of State volunteers, mostly settlers, who had their private grievances and revenges. He concentrated his army of regulars at Fort Vancouver, used a part of them for the protection of friendly Indians against white aggressors, and disposed the remainder so as to render warfare intelligent and void of brutality. But the State volunteers made campaigns on their own responsibility and with continued loss of prestige. The bitterness between the policies of extermination and of civilized warfare was nearly as great as that between the red and white foemen. As a result of the clash between the two policies, neither regulars nor volunteers did anything of importance, while the Indians secured several successes.

On February 22d, 1856, while the volunteers were attending a " Washington Birthday ball" on Rogue River, they were surprised, and Captain Wright and 23 others were killed. All the ranches on the river were sacked and burned. Later on, General Wool got his forces in hand. He passed the Cascades of the Columbia on his way to the Dalles, leaving at the Middle Cascades a small force. Scarcely had he passed, when the Indians attacked this force, protected by the block house there, and kept up an unequal battle for a day and a night, murdering, meanwhile, all the citizens they found in exposed places. Word of this "Cascade Massacre" reached Colonel Wright, in command of the advanced forces, and he returned to find that even the friendly Cascade Indians had turned against the whites and had induced the massacre. The leaders were tried by court martial and hung.

Colonel Wright then advanced again, leaving a stronger force at the Cascades, under Lieutenant Phil. Sheridan. Colonel Wright soon met the hostiles, of many tribes and in a force estimated at 1,200 warriors. His own force did not exceed 475 effectives, but it was well supplied and held a position which cut the Indians off from the river and the lands they had depended on for subsistance. Neither party cared to risk an open engagement. The summer passed in a series of parleys, in which many chiefs surrendered and agreed to live in peace.

The troops in the south were pursuing a similar policy, though with a more pugnacious foe. Chief John's band of Rogue Rivers surrounded Captain Smith's force of 90 men, supported by a howitzer, and would have compelled their surrender, with the massacre it implied, had not a timely reinforcement come to the rescue and dashed into the besiegers, routing them with heavy loss. All the while, the friendly Indians were being gathered on to reservations, which began to grow in favor as an asylum for such hostiles as were tired of warfare. John's band surrendered on condition that it should escape punishment and be given a place on a reservation. This action was followed by a surrender of nearly all the Lower Rogue Rivers on the same terms. The northern tribes caught the spirit of surrender and readily found places on lands dedicated to them forever. Military stations were established among the tribes, each well equipped and officered, and with instructions to deal firmly but justly with all within their jurisdiction.

By 1857 peace reigned throughout the Oregon region, and more had been accomplished toward bringing it about in the last year than in the two years before. While the loss of life had not been as great as in some other Indian wars, the destruction of property had been enormous. Costly as it had been to the settlers, it was even more so to the Government.

Chapter VI.

WAR WITH THE CHEYENNES.

THE Arrapahoes are native to that immense tract east of the mountains and between the Platte and Arkansas Rivers. The Cheyennes were driven into the same region from the east of the Mississippi by the powerful Sioux. The Sioux themselves came to occupy the country north of the Platte. All of these tribes are strong and warlike. They are made up of several smaller tribes, the Sioux alone embracing seven families or tribes.

From the earliest days of settlement west of the Mississippi these Indians made war on the whites. In 1841 a battle between trappers and the combined warriors of the Cheyennes and Sioux was fought on Snake River, with terrible loss on both sides. Fremont, on his several expeditions, found them hostile, but avoided trouble by threatening them with the vengeance of the "Great Father" in case they molested him. In 1845, Colonel Kearney awed them into good behavior by an ostentatious parade of his dragoons

WAR WITH THE CHEYENNES.

and howitzers. In 1847, the Kiowas, Apaches, Pawnees and Comanches were in coalition against the whites. They asked the Cheyennes to join, but they were intimidated by the timely arrival of two cavalry companies under Colonel Gilpin.

In 1854 a coalition was formed of Cheyennes and Arrapahoes, and war broke out, begun by the Sioux. The first engagement was with Lieutenant Grattan and his command near Fort Laramie. A force of Brule-Sioux warriors under their chief, Bear, were fired upon by Grattans's, soldiers who in turn were exterminated. The Indians menaced Fort Laramie for a few days, but departed on the arrival of reinforcements from Fort Riley; Bear was killed, and his successor was Little Thunder, a daring chief, who never failed to strike the whites a blow when opportunity occurred. He destroyed several mail parties and killed Captain Gibson and many of his men. In 1855, General Harney marched from Fort Leavensworth with 1300 men to the scene of hostilities. The General was an uncompromising Indian hater and fighter, and he came to teach them a lesson. He reached Fort Kearney in safety, and continued his journey to Ash Hollow, where he learned that the Brules were encamped in force. Harney prepared for an attack. He sent a cavalry force to cut off the rear of the Indian forces, and then advanced with his infantry. When Little Thunder came forward to parley, Harney received him coldly. Little Thunder returned to his warriors, who soon discovered that their retreat was cut off. Amid the commotion which followed this discovery, Harney ordered his infantry to advance firing. They dashed forward with wild yells, and mowed down the Indians as they rushed onward. The Indian forces could not withstand the furious onset and broke fleeing to the bluff, leaving behind all their traps. The cavalry pursued them and kept them in disastrous flight for eight or ten miles, killing many. The Indian losses numbered over an hundred, many of whom were women and children. Their loss of tents, provisions, robes and utensils was total. Such a blow had never been struck at these powerful tribes of the plains and the lesson was valuable. They surrendered the murderers they were harboring, and agreed to be peaceable in the future. Harney was censured for killing women and children, but justified himself in the eyes of his accusers, and was promoted by President Buchanan.

Though this blow crushed the Sioux, it had no effect on the Cheyennes and Arrapahoes. The Kansas political troubles were now on, and the troops were needed in that Territory in 1856.

Immunity from punishment made these tribes bolder. They kept up constant war on emigrants and mail parties. At length a company under Captain Stuart met a marauding force near Fort Kearney and defeated it with heavy loss. This seemed to incite the Indians to worse barbarities, and attacks and murders were frequent all through 1856. In 1857 a large cavalry force under Colonel Sumner was sent against them. He came upon a force of 300 Indians in the Valley of Solomon's Fork, and immediately charged them. The Indians broke and fled, but escaped after a five-mile chase, owing to the freshness and fleetness of their ponies. The losses on either side were not heavy, but the effect of the scare was to break the Indian force up into small parties and thus prevent danger from organized action.

There was comparative quiet in the Cheyenne and Arrapahoe region for two or three years, when the Government was relieved of all responsibility for keeping peace, by the arrival of settlers. The cry of gold discovery in the Rockies brought thither a flood of adventurers, similar to the influx into California in 1849. These promiscuous and rude adventurers commanded a respect from the Indians which the Government could not enforce. Inside of three years, there were 80,000 whites in the Pike's Peak country, far too many to fear organized war on the part of the Indians, yet, strange to say, of a kind of whom the Indians never complained. It may be that their engagements in the past with the forces of the United States, had impressed them with the futility of contending against skill and numbers, but it is more than likely that geography had more to do with it than force. The gold hunters occupied the region which divided the mountain tribes from those of the plain, so that hostiles on either side sought their friendship and thus acquired arms and ammunition with which to fight each other.

In 1861, the Cheyennes and Arrapahoes made a celebrated treaty with the Government in which they gave away the most desirable of their lands to Colorado settlers, and in addition the right of the public to lay out roads and highways across their own lands. They never dreamed that they had given the right to build a railroad through their country. But when the Kansas Pacific projectors began to invade the reserve lands with its rails, a new cause of hostility was found, and the troubles of 1864 began.

Chapter VII.

NAVAJO HOSTILITIES.

THE Navajos dwell in the northwest angle of New Mexico and the northeast angle of Arizona. They were ascribed to the fierce Apaches by the Spaniards, but are really a link between them and the better civilized Pueblos, if not descendants of the latter. They are a well proportioned, finely grown, fair countenanced people, who dwell in grass covered huts, and devote themselves to pasturage and crude agriculture. They dress better than the average Indian and go armed with lance and shield very like ancient Grecians or Romans. They manufacture all their clothing and blankets, and the latter are a wonder for beauty of design and artistic finish. They are acquainted with the smelting of metals and the production of pottery.

In war they do not scalp an enemy, and in taste are like the Jews in the respect that they abhor bear and hog meat. They respect their wives, and womankind is not subject to drudgery as with other Indians, though young girls unite the part of shepherd with that of weaving. Their only god, Whai-la-hay, is a female, to whom their knowledge of weaving and pottery is due. The one condition of salvation is that the deceased has treated his wife well. They numbered 20,000 beings when their territory was acquired by the United States, and 2,000 warriors. They had no government, but seemed to be an aggregation of peaceful families, each left to do as it pleased. When our Government came to treat with them it found nothing to treat with, and when it imposed such terms as seemed necessary for future amicable relations there was no body to make it binding. Moreover they indulged the infatuation that they were superior in numbers to the white race. In addition they had fought Spaniards and Mexicans for centuries and with success. Under all these conditions it was easy for the United States to make a mistake in dealing with them. This mistake it did make when General Kearney assumed that in conquering New Mexico, and engaging in general stipulations he had also treated with the Navajos.

While a detachment of our troops were visiting the Rio Grande region, magnifying their strength and sealing treaties with a show of force, they were suddenly swooped down upon by the

Navajos and deprived of all their cattle and stores. This audacity called for an expedition against them. It entered their country in two columns and forced them into submission without bloodshed; but it no sooner left than every Navajo felt at liberty to do as he pleased again. In 1847 another expedition was sent against them, but it did not even succeed in making a treaty. In 1848, another was sent which simply repeated the experience of the first. In 1849, a fourth expedition was fitted out, accompanied by a force of 150 friendly Navajos. It joined battle with the hostiles in the Canon de Chelly, the result of which was the death of a leading chief and several warriors. A treaty was made, but it proved no more binding than former ones. They were at large again as soon as force failed to confront them.

In 1852 Colonel Sumner marched against them and built Fort Defiance in the heart of their country. This was a master stroke. It impressed them with the resources of the whites, and secured peace for two years. But the plundering habits of the tribe reasserted themselves, and they grew to be as big a nuisance as ever. The tribe as a whole was not to blame, for having no internal government it could not restrain its vicious members, as its better portion desired.

Its marauders finally grew bold enough to carry their depredations and even their murders to the very limits of the Fort. Having gathered about it in numbers, they were attacked by the troops under Colonel Miles and driven off. Colonel Miles then pursued them and carried consternation through the Navajo country. He was attacked in the Canon de Chelly by Indians on the summits, but they could do no harm with their arrows. At the mouth of the canon he was met by Chief Nak-risk-thaw-nee, with proposals of peace. The answer was, " no peace until every Navajo murderer is delivered over for trial." The troops moved on, capturing sheep and devastating corn-fields, and finally returned to the Fort loaded with booty. It was thought that this devastating warfare would prove more effective than the killing of the foe. But they were prepared to stand it, for a while at least.

Soon after another expediton of 60 men started out under Captain Hatch. It came up with the Indians under Sarcillo Largo and battle was joined. The fighting was fierce for a time but finally the chief fell and his followers fled, leaving behind six dead warriors and all their camp effects. This was the first battle in which the Navajos were known to use firearms, which they handled awkwardly. The Mormons were held responsible for having furnished them with these improved weapons.

Word now came in that the Navajos had been induced by the Mormons to join the Pi-Utes in a war of extermination against the Americans. Colonel Miles, therefore, started on a scout with 300 men, and on the first day came on a body of hostiles which he dispersed, capturing their horses and sheep. A detachment of 126 men was sent to attack Ka-ya-ta-na's camp in a canon fifteen miles distant. They charged down the steep sides of the canon, stampeded the Indians, and captured 20 horses and 4000 sheep.

It was now clear that the Navajos could not be reduced by numbers, for no numbers could be effective in their broken country. The hostiles could not be brought to a stand and they were agile in escape. But they were usually accompanied by their herds and of these they could be deprived. They were also dependent on their fields of wheat and vegetables, and these could be destroyed. So it was determined to keep up a series of expeditions against them and give them no time for repose. With this object in view Major Brook circled through their country, fighting often, but having only one pitched battle, in which the Indians lost 25 warriors. In return for this the Navajos attacked the front herd and succeeded in killing two men and running away with 64 horses and mules. This induced Colonel Miles to start with 260 soldiers and 150 volunteer Zuni against the hostiles, who were found and attacked, with the loss of few men and the capture of 250 horses. A similar expedition under Lieut. Howland made even a larger capture.

More extensive scouts were planned and ready to start, when the Navajos sued for peace. This kind of warfare was more than they could stand, they could not be ever running about to escape destruction, while their flocks and means of subsistance were being gradually lost to them. Satisfactory terms were agreed upon and such a peace as could be had with the disjointed Navajos was ratified.

This peace lasted, with unimportant interruptions, till 1861, when it was broken by the fight at Fort Fauntleroy. This was a scrimmage between the soldiers and Indians at a horse race, at which animosities were engendered which led to an attack by the soldiers and a massacre of several Navajos, including their women and children. When it was seen that the soldiers were to blame peace messengers were sent to the Indians, but they returned with the response that the Navajos had given them a severe flogging. This of course meant war. A force was sent against them and a battle ensued, in which the hostiles suffered severely. A temporary peace was patched up, only to be broken by raids and stealings; to all requests to come to permanent terms they invariablly answered, "You," (the whites), " keep us in such a state of tumult, we cannot raise cattle or crops on which to live, therefore we are forced to steal." In a year (1861-62), they drove off 100,000 head of sheep, 1,000 head of cattle, besides horses and mules. They also killed many persons without regard to age or sex.

In September, 1862, a formidable militia force was organized against them, with a view to extermination, but its operations were checked by the Government, because such a force never stopped to discriminate between friendly and hostile Indians. At length General Carleton decided to apply the reservation policy; he said, " they have no internal Government with which to make a treaty binding. They are patriarchal like Abraham of old, one set of families may promise, another may violate. They understand force, but if force be removed they become lawless. They should be collected in groups away from their mountains and hiding places, and should be taught to read and write, and to know the truths of Christianity." Bravely said, but the difficulty was to get at these agile people, or if that were possible, to separate the hostiles from the peaceful. He notified them of his project, and gave them till a certain day to accept, all who failed were to be regarded as hostile.

A large number accepted. Against the rest troops were ordered to operate. Every marauding expedition of Navajos was followed up by troops, with orders to kill all warriors in arms, and to hold women and children as captives. These orders were strictly obeyed. But such was the agility of the Indians that only one of their parties, of 130 members, was captured in 1863, notwithstanding the fact that the famous Kit Carson had a host of troopers at his back. It was decided that really little could be done till winter, when they would be forced to seek the security of the canons for the purpose of saving their stock. Their great rendezvous would then be the Canon de Chelly, one of the most remarkable natural wonders in the United States, its approaches being secure and its walls lined by ancient cliff-dwellings.

For this Canon Colonel Carson started in Jan. 1864, with 390 men, having sent one company to operate from the eastern end. After a hard march through the snow, they reached the canon and attacked the guard to its approach, killing eleven

Indians and capturing several squaws and children. He then disposed his forces so that they might descend the canon, but was surprised to find that the force destined for the eastern entrance had traversed the entire length of it, without even so much as a battle, the enemy having taken the alarm and scampered to the heights through ways known only to themselves. Still the effect of the expedition was fully felt by the hostiles. They were on the borders of starvation and ready for terms. The only conditions were that they should consent to removal to the reservation at the Bosque. These terms were readily accepted and Carson's expedition was practically at an end. Carson's command consisted af 2,000 picked men. He chose the right season for his expedition and used his forces so as to hem the hostiles in completely. Their surrender was almost as a nation. In a single magnificent operation, and with the killing of but few, he gathered in 10,000 Indians—the largest single capture on record. Those who remained out quickly responded to the, now well known, overtures, and the resources of the Government were taxed to the uttermost to find support for them. Fort Canby was disbanded in August and Kit Carson was sent to the plains to fight Kiowas and Comanches, and the Navajo wars were at an end.

These interesting Indians had tried the experiment of reservation life in good faith, but they had become dissatisfied with the repeated failure of their crops. In 1868, General Sherman and Colonel Tappan visited them as a Peace Commission. They report that the reservation of Bosque Redondo had been badly chosen, owing to its sterility of soil, and that no agriculturist could make a living there. They recommended that the Navajos be removed to a reservation nearer their old home and with better advantages. This was done, and since then their condition has steadily improved. In 1876 the Navajos were reported as self-supporting. Since then they have been given additional lands. owing to increase in population and herds.

Chapter VIII.

THE AFFAIR OF MOUNTAIN MEADOW.

THE Indians who lived in the great Utah Basin or who used it as part of their tramping grounds, were of the Shoshone stock, and embraced the Snake, Bannock and Ute families. These families were again sub-divided into tribes with various names, more or less fanciful. As a rule, they were not unfriendly to the whites, though not disinclined to war under the provocations which frequently arose. The Mormons had no trouble with them, because they approached them as equals and without a desire to force their civilization upon them. They had great power over them, for the reason that they stood up for them, when the United States attempted to execute its authority among them. It may be said that the Mormon influence over them was bad, in so far as it represented antagonism to the Government.

It is not our purpose to narrate how bitter Mormon antagonism became in 1856, nor to discuss the wisdom of that costly and useless invasion of their country by the Army of the United States, but this invasion produced the greatest excitement in all Mormondom. It fanned the flames of religious and political passion till they broke out in various forms. In that year there passed through Salt Lake a large emigrant train, composed mostly of Arkansas families, on their way to Southern California. These emigrants encamped for several days at Salt Lake where their numbers were largely increased by Gentile accessions, and by some Mormons who had become dissatisfied with their religion.

When the emigrant train started on, it was denied supplies in the Mormon settlements, was treated as an intrusive and dangerous mass, and was denounced as the vanguard of such an eastern mob as might soon be expected to come for the purpose of sacking the Mormon Zion. The train moved rapidly, amid contumely and scant food supply, but without thought of direct attack on their lives. After crossing the Great Basin, they stopped for rest at Mountain Meadows, in Southwestern Utah. While enjoying their rest here, their camp was suddenly attacked by Indians, who fired upon the emigrants as they were seated around their fires cooking breakfast. Seven of their number fell in death at the first volley, and sixteen were wounded. The rest were thrown into confusion, but quickly rallied, and having placed their women and children under shelter of the wagons, they were soon returning the fire with deadly effect. The Indians recoiled, and were held to their bloody work with difficulty by their leaders, several of whom were recognized as whites in disguise. They shot down the cattle of the emigrants, and maintained a desultory fire throughout the day and night.

On the next day the Indians were reinforced, and by whites in diguise, supposably Mormon allies. The emigrants, meanwhile, were making their position strong by chaining their wagons together and banking earth against them. Two of their number stole out of the valley and started to Cedar City for aid. They met three citizens of Cedar City on their way, and were attacked by them. One of them was instantly killed and the other wounded. The wounded man made his way back to the emigrant camp, and his story revealed the awful fact that whites as well as Indians were their antagonists. In this they were confirmed by witnessing a manoeuvering party on the divide of the Meadows, composed of fully 250 men, one third of whom were whites. This party decided that the position of the emigrants was impregnable.

But, surrounded as they were, escape was out of the question. Surrender must be a matter of only a few days. A council of Mormons had been held and it was agreed that the emigrants should be decoyed from their stronghold and exterminated. Lee and Bateman, two Mormon leaders, approached the camp with a flag of truce. Lee represented to the emigrants that the Indians were very excited and bent on massacre, but that he had gotten them to promise they would injure no one who surrendered to the Mormons. Believing that the Mormons would protect them, the surrender was made. The men were to march out unarmed, each one with a Mormon by his side, to make the Indians believe he was a captive. The wagons, loaded with food, sick and wounded were to go ahead. The women and children were to follow. The procession passed over the divide in the Meadows and down the slope beyond. A Mormon leader, Higbee, is there with a company of militia. His appearance is assuring, for his company may prove a source of protection in case the Indians renew hostilities. But in a twinkling his company wheels, and each member aims for the emigrant nearest him. Flash go their rifles in concert and down drop the victims of their bullets. The Indians rush from their ambush and dash with yells upon the women. The horrid work goes on upon the right and left, Lee being present everywhere to see that the extermination is made complete. The rifle, the tomahawk, the bowie-knife, all do their devilish bidding, till there is no one left to tell the tale of a massacre whose fiendishness is without parallel. If it be said it was not inspired by white men, and not participated in by them, the answer is, no Indian could be so hellishly malignant, however much he might be a tool and dupe. The men all fell at the first fire. The wounded and the women were brained with tomahawks. Some 18 children, too young to babble as witnesses, were taken and distributed among the Mormon families. The property of the emigrants was divided, one part went to the Indians, the other was sold for the benefit of the Mormon Church. The date of the massacre was Sept. 11, 1857.

For months and years this massacre gave occasion for discussion and investigation. The Mormon leaders charged it to the Indians, who had been excited by the hostility of the whites. Even admitting that whites had participated in it they too had been wronged. The Church, as a Church, had nothing to do with it. On the other hand, it was contended that the whole thing was actuated by the Church, and bore evidence of its action. The facts never could be conclusively reached, for the Mormons had hushed the lips of those who might have convicted them, with their bullets.

In 1859 Captain Campbell passed through the Meadows and buried the remains of 120 men, women and children. The Mormons showered honors upon Lee and the other leaders in this dastardly affair. Years afterwards they were brought to trial. The first trial was a farce. The second one was even a worse farce, in the respect that the shrewder Mormons felt that Lee must be sacrificed in order to save themselves. He was found guilty of murder, and was shot to death on the scene of the massacre, where he confessed to having killed five of the emigrants with his own hands. He died cursing the leaders who had deserted him, but professing faith in his religion. He was not a victim to justice, but was as much murdered by his accomplices as if they had fired the last fatal volley.

Chapter IX.

THE SPOKANE WARS.

IN 1858, the Spokanes and other tribes in Washington Territory grew uneasy over the approach of white settlers in the neighborhood of the Colville mines. Though they could safely boast that they had never shed the blood of white men, an expedition against them was deemed necessary. Colonel Steptoe started with 157 men and two howitzers for the Spokane. When crossing the prairie which borders the Ingossomen Creek, he was suddenly confronted by 1,200 warriors—Spokanes, Pelouses, Coeur d' Allenes and Yakimas. They tried to provoke an attack, but the Colonel avoided a collision till he found the cover of a ravine. Here he held a conference which ended in satisfactory explanations. This was what the Colonel most needed, for it gave him opportunity for a safe and honorable retreat.

But it so happened that an impulsive Chief, Mil-kap-si, had not been consulted, he rushed upon the Colonel's rear guard with his band and opened fire. The fire became general on the part of the Indians, and many of the white troops fell. Colonel Steptoe was forced to relinquish retreat and form for battle. He did so, on the most advantageous spot he could find, but only to be surrounded on three sides by Indians, Spokanes on the north, Coeur d' Allenes on the east, and Pelouses on the west, all of whom kept up an incessant firing. At night-fall it was decided that the position could not be defended, and that safety lay only in stealthy and rapid retreat. The howitzer and useless guns were buried, the wounded stock was killed, all provisions and accoutrements, except what each soldier could lightly carry, were abandoned. Under cover of the darkness the soldiers filed down the hill at the rear, and plunged off in rapid flight, never stopping till they reached the Snake river, 90 miles below.

This affair threw the settlements into the greatest consternation, for the fact that so peaceful a nation as the Spokanes had uprisen, gave evidence of a great grievance and a general war. Investigation showed that the Indians had been influenced by the Mormon statement that Jesus Christ had appeared eastward of the mountains, and his coming might soon be expected on the westward. Accordingly, General Clarke, Commander on the Pacific, issued orders that all Indians be detached from Mormon influence. This was all the more necessary, because the Indians were found to be well provided with arms and ammunition, which they could have gotten only from Mormon traders, or from the posts of the Hudson Bay Company. Investigation also showed that the Indians were dissatisfied with the failure of the Government to approve and carry out the various treaties which had been lately made. This was true of the friendly Indians; but, on the other hand, the wilder tribes, were opposed to any and all treaties, for they felt they would curtail their privileges.

So discontent, whose sources were both within and without, grew apace. The conviction arose that the Indians must be punished and General Clarke prepared for this. His ultamatum was that the Spokanes and other friendly tribes drive all the hostiles from their midst, restore the property taken from Colonel Steptoe, and surrender all who fired on his command without the consent of the chiefs. The reply came that they did not want to fight, but would not deliver up their neighbors. Colonel Wright moved with the main column of the gathered forces from Fort Walla Walla. Another column had its base at Fort Simcoe on the Yakima. A treaty was made with the Nez Perces, and 30 of their number inlisted as volunteers. Wright's column moved with 570 regulars, 30 Indian scouts, 100 teamsters and two howitzers. They built Fort Taylor on the Snake, and garrisoned it. The main body again marched to Four Lakes, where they found the Indians in force. Colonel Wright threw two companies in the rear and charged their front with four other companies. The Indians fled over the hill and across the plain beyond, many of their number being shot down by the riflemen who had gained the cover of a small piece of woods.

The pursuit was kept up the next day, and the Indians were found again in front of a stretch of timber, they having set the prairie grass on fire to stop their pursuers. Under cover of the smoke they opened fire on the troops. A charge through the flames was ordered and the Indians were forced into the timber. The howitzers opened on them and they were forced to flee, being pursued closely by the troops. For seven hours the running fight was kept up and the distance traversed was 14 miles. The troops did not suffer much from the Indian fire, but the Indians lost two of their chiefs and many warriors.

The Indians were much discouraged and called for a parley. Col. Wright demanded absolute surrender. Some of the chiefs favored it, and brought in the offenders in their tribe. Others opposed. The Col. then continued his pursuit up the Spokane. He found that parties of Indians were running their stock off into the mountains. These he attacked and captured 800 horses. This was a worse blow to the Indians than a victorious battle would have proved, for horses were almost their sole wealth.

Col. Wright next moved across to the mission on Coeur d' Allene River, where he met 400 Indians in council. Here his conditions of surrender were accepted. He then marched to Lahto, where he met the Spokanes in council. They were treated with on the same terms as the Coeur d' Allenes, and gave promises of permanent good behavior. Meanwhile Major Garnett had fought a victorious battle on the Yakima with the Pelouses, and had brought them to terms. In all these treaties Col. Wright insisted strenuously on the surrender of those Indians who had offended the laws of their tribe and the country, by waging war without the consent of their chiefs, by murdering and pillaging and by stealing cattle. He secured a large number of culprits in this way and had them properly punished. This campaign, so effective of peace, was remarkable in the fact that it embraced, two battles, several skirmishes, the loss of many Indian warriors, the capture of over 1000 horses, the destruction of large quantities of Indian supplies, the punishment by death of 14 murderers and robbers, the surrender of three powerful tribes, the giving of numerous hostages for good behavior, all without the loss of a single white soldier killed in battle.

CHAPTER X.

THE FIERCE APACHES AND ARRAPAHOES.

THE Apaches have resisted the whites more stubbornly than any other Indian tribe. They have had desert, rock and mountain to aid them. They have proven brave, cunning and fleet. There is no atrocity they have not committed and none they have not been subjected to. They have terrorized a country larger than five average States and have come to be regarded as the most savage and treacherous dwellers on the soil of the United States.

They originally embraced nine tribes, or families, whose territory was in New Mexico and Arizona, with margins south into Mexico and north to the Ute country. The Mexicans never gained any control over the Apaches, with whom they were perpetually at war. Apaches were always a terror to emigrants passing over the southern routes to California. They never attacked but by surprise. Yet when settlers first went into New Mexico to stop permanently, strange to say, the Apaches let them alone, for they saw in them prospective allies against the Mexicans, whom they mortally hated.

In 1851 the Apaches murdered a mail party of 11 men. The offending band was captured and isolated on a reservation. In 1853, they attacked and almost annihilated Lieutenant Davidson's command of 60 men. Immediately a large force of troops was thrown into the midst of the offending tribe and it was forced to sue for peace. In 1854-55 the Government was at war with the Apaches, southeast of the Rio Grande, who surrendered only after receiving severe punishment.

The eastern Apaches made no general war on the United States till the outbreak of the Southern Rebellion, but the western Apaches seemed never to cease their marauding expeditions and piratical warfare. At the opening of our civil war the troops were withdrawn from the Apache country, and the mail routes were abandoned. The western Apaches took advantage of the situation and ran wild in their robberies and murders. They seemed to be everywhere and men and women were killed and ranches destroyed, even where settlements were thick. The mining town of Tubac was deserted and Tucson dwindled away to a village of 200 people.

To add to the desperation of the situation the Texas militia invaded New Mexico and the Apache country in the interest of the South. They occupied Fort Stanton, and made their conquest of the country complete for a time. But the Utes and Jicarilla Apaches turned against them. Soon the Mescalero Apaches revolted and carried on predatory war against the Confederates and all settlers. This condition would have proved ruinous to New Mexico and Arizona, but for the fact that Colorado volunteers so augmented the forces of General Canby, that he was able to drive the Texans from the line of the Rio Grande. At the same time General Carleton was pushing a column of 3,000 Californians eastward from Fort Yuma and opening communications with the Pacific coast. He met with desperate resistance on the part of the western Apaches who made a stand at Apache Pass, which they thought impregnable. But the fire of Carleton's mountain howitzers demoralized them and they fled with a loss of 66 killed.

In September, 1862, Carleton reached the Rio Grande and relieved Canby. He now devoted his entire attention to the subjugation of the Indians. He sent Kit Carson, with five companies, to Fort Stanton to operate against the Mescaleros and Navajos. Capt. McCleave was sent directly into the Mescalero-Apache country. Capt. Roberts, was sent to the same section by another route. The troops were nearly all Californians, with no love for Indians, especially Apaches. They were under orders to "kill the men wherever found and to take all women and children prisoners."

Carson reached Fort Stanton without much fighting. McCleave encountered the Apaches at Dog Canon, one of their strongholds, and completely routed a force of 100 warriors, who beat a retreat to Fort Stanton and surrendered to Kit Carson. The chief of this band was "Always Ready," who surrendered with the following speech: "You are stronger than we. We have fought you so long as we had rifles and powder; but your weapons are better than ours. Give us like weapons and turn us loose and we will fight you again. But we are worn out; we have no heart, no provisions, no means to live. Your troops are everywhere. Our springs are either occupied or overlooked by your men. You have driven us from our last and best stronghold and we have no more heart. Do with us as seems good to you, but do not forget that we are men and braves." His band was sent to the reservation at Bosque Redondo, and it was voluntarily followed by hundreds of others of the Mescalero-Apaches.

The attention of the army was now turned to the Mimbreno-Apaches. During the early part of 1863, more than forty of their warriors were killed. The latter part of the year was devoted to conquest of the Navajos. So actively had operations been carried on that the Navajos surrendered almost as a tribe, and in a single year over 5000 of them were placed on the Bosque reservation.

In 1864, General Carleton was free to direct all his energies against the Western Apaches. He had made up his mind that nothing but a war of extermination would settle these marauders. They moved so rapidly and eluded pursuit so successfully by running over the Mexican border, that Carleton asked the co-operation of the Governors of Sonora and Chihuahua, which was promised. The miners of the respective mining towns in Arizona agreed to keep a force in the field. The Pimas and Maricopas were armed with improved weapons and furnished with white officers. Here was a combination of foreign and home military, armed miners and two friendly Indian tribes against the Apaches, and all intent on a war of extermination. Carleton said: "the work must be done now and effectually, or we shall have a twenty years, war on our hands."

So, at it they went. The Apaches had the help of the Navajos, who yet remained unsubdued. The war was carried on by both sides with unrelenting fury. Battle after battle was fought, with great loss of life. The loss to our troops was never fully reported, but as to the enemy the results of the year's work footed as follows:— Indians killed 363, wounded 140, sheep captured 12,284, horses 2,742. Over 2,000 Navajos were sent to the Bosque reservation, but the wily Apaches avoided capture. They were neither exterminated nor conquered, though the losses of crops in their sheltered valleys had made them poor and disposed them to peace.

The Apache bosom burned against the one condition of surrender which banished them to the Bosque reservation. They agreed to treat, but not with this alternative as a stipulation. They sent four of their chiefs to inspect this reservation and report to the tribe, but none of them returned, and the war went on. At the close of the Civil War in the United States, New Mexico fell into the Department of Missouri, and Arizona into that of the Pacific. General Halleck had command in the latter Department, and he believed fully in the policy of exterminating the Apaches, who were now mostly in Arizona. "It is useless to negotiate with them," he said, "for they will observe no treaties, agreements or truces. With them there is no alternative but vigorous war, till they are completely destroyed or forced to surrender as prisoners of war."

The troops in Arizona were under the command of General Mason, and he prosecuted the war on the Apaches even more relentlessly than before. The white soldiers and citizens excelled the Indians in cruelty, and to kill an Indian, on general principles, was the comman law of the situation. The unprovoked murder of Waba Yuma, chief of the Hualapais, drove that friendly tribe into hostility, and they proved to be far more vicious warriors than the Apaches. The Bosque reservation was only designed for temporary use. Most of the Indians on it had been sent there with the promise that they would be provided with larger and permanent reservations. The crops failed at the Bosque in 1865. The Navajos and Apaches did not agree. Each element claimed the early fulfillment of the Government promise. Each charged the agent at the reservation with favoritism. In November 1865 the entire tribe of Mescalero-Apaches left the reservation and went to their own country. This meant war, and White Eye fought his tribe for several years. When it finally surrendered, it got a reservation of its own in its own country.

As the Apache wars continued the Indians found out new covers in the mountain fastnesses, and their abandoned valleys were occupied by the whites. Deserted towns and villages were repopulated and the mining camps became comparatively safe. Still, the roads and trails were full of danger, and no one dared venture far from a peopled center without arms. Cattle were run off by the Indians from farm and ranche. There was no telling the moment when these swift marauders would appear. Years of war had only added to their cunning and their malice. Not a single Apache had been thoroughly subdued, except when mortally shot. The policy of extermination had been thoroughly tried, and at the beginning of 1869, many of the army officers were free to confess that it was a failure.

In April 1869, a permanent Board of Indian Commissioners was formed. It advised a change from a forceful to a peaceful policy in dealing with the Indians. But General Ord, who had come into command on the Pacific, pursued the policy of extermination. In that year, he reported that 200 Apaches had been killed by parties who had trailed them into their mountain fastnesses. Many of their villages had been burned and large quantities of stores destroyed. While he was disproving the wisdom of his own policy, the object of legitimate war was being obtained. The Indians were learning that they could not escape the invading power of the whites, nor forever submit to destruction of their property. One tribe of Arivapas came in and surrendered to Lieutenant Whitman, at camp Grant, and there being no reservation for them to go to, he set them to work cutting hay for the garrison. In April they were set upon by Americans, Mexicans and Papago Indians from Tucson and practically exterminated, women and children being butchered as well as the men. This Camp Grant massacre raised a whirlwind of excitement among all humanitarians, and President Grant sent Vincent Colyer to the scene, with power to abjust the Indian troubles. He was not welcomed by the whites of Arizona, and knew nothing of Indin nature—at least Apache nature. Yet he worked heroically, laid out an extensive plan of reservations, and was instrumental in securing the removal of many tribes to them. Their site was generally illy chosen and the occupants lived discontentedly. Many of them were afterwards abandoned by the Indians, who left altogether or were transferred to more favorable sites.

In 1871 General Crook took command in Arizona. He was a noted Indian fighter but not an exterminator. He believed in conquering and then treating justly. He said, "I am satisfied that a sharp, active campaign against the Apache will make him one of the best Indians in the country and save the government millions of dollars. He must either cultivate the soil or steal. Our vacillating policy encourages him to the latter." Colyer was there and was given time to try his peace policy. Crook was then given full power to proceed, but not wishing to clash with the peace commissioners he contented himself with pursuing and punishing, without prosecuting active hostiles.

At length the Colyer policy was pronounced a failure. The hostiles neither came in nor remained quiet. They made 54 attacks in the year 1872, killing over 50 citizens and soldiers and stealing 500 horses. Crook then announced his intention of punishing the incorrigably hostile. He began operations in a country where the enemy was imbued with the hatreds of three centuries, where whites were almost as barbarous as the Apaches, where criminals from other States and Territories had sought refuge, where continuous war had doubled savagery, where mountain and ravine made pursuit difficult, where escape over the Mexican border was easy and final. His winter campaign against the Tontos, Coyoteros, Tampais, and Hualapais, brought them to terms. All of these had fooled Colyer and his peace notions. They were once more placed on reservations, where they still remain, except as they were changed for health considerations.

Crook fought Apache with Apache. He enlisted every friendly he could and thus pursued with a knowledge the whites could never have acquired in themselves. His employment of Indian police at reservations has since been generally adopted. The Apaches were impressed with the information that their welfare lay in their own keeping. By making these democratic people agents of the law, they were led to punish their own evil doers. This was a mighty stride forward. A new era had dawned on the Apaches. Whenever they were friendly they were useful. Only the renegades were left to be hunted. In 1875 Governor Safford said in his message: "At no period in the history of Arizona have our Indian affairs been so satisfactory. General Crook, in the subjugation of the Apaches, has sustained his former well-earned military reputation and deserves the gratitude of our people." No extermination, no peace; neither vengeance nor sentimentalism; justice to white and red:— this was the Crook policy.

But in 1874 the reservations of Arizona passed from the War Department to the Indian Bureau. The policy of the latter was that of concentration. It began to take from the Indians their promised future homes, the homes they had improved, the lands they had irrigated. Crook refused to countenance this injustice, and was removed. Colonel Kautz succeeded him, but held to Crook's views in a modified way. The Indian Bureau continued its shifting of Indians from old to new agencies. Force was used by these advocates of peace to effect their object. The upshot of the new dispensation was discontent among the whole of the tribes, desertion from the reservations, more grinding tyranny on the part of the Bureau, revolt on the part of the Indians.

By 1878, there was a general breaking up of all that had been previously established. The Apaches were abroad in bands, and as predatory and dangerous as ever. Every dissatisfied Indian helped to augment the forces that skimmed the Mexican borders, now here, killing and stealing; now there, burning and murdering. In 1879, Major Morrow hunted them incessantly with the 9th Cavalry but they dodged him with the acumen of the fox in front of the hounds. In 1880, Colonel Hatch chased them through all the recesses of the San Mates, Mimbres and Mogollon mountains, and Colonel Carr met them only to turn them south into Mexico. In this long and desperate chase, the Indians had no friends and were desperate. They killed and plundered indiscriminately, and whatever their own losses may have been they left a three-fold loss in their trail.

The hostile Apache in Mexico was out of the way of American troops, but was not much better off. He was dangerous wherever he might be, and therefore an object of hatred. But with the Mexican side we have nothing to do. The Apache returned quick enough and gave our forces something to do. His return, however, set people to thinking. Might there not be a mistake in dealing with him. For a man—even an Indian man—to say: "I would sooner die than be on such or such an reservation, where I shall only perish with disease or starvation, might there not be provided a congenial reservation. Since the claim of the white man was only a theft any way, why might not there be consideration enough to say to the Indian 'enjoy the slice we leave you.'"

In 1882, a treaty was concluded with Mexico which authorized the pursuit of Indians by the troops of the two nationalities across the borders. At the same time General Crook was returned to his old command in Arizona. He had common sense, and kept faith with the Indians. For these things they liked him, though many whites did not. The biggest surrender of the year was that of the Indian Bureau to General Crook. He persuaded the discontented Indians to go back to reservations and he took care to see that they were where they could be happy and useful. He next turned his attention to the hostiles, mostly over the border in Mexico. They had no homes and were incorrigible. They refused every offer to negotiate. Yet they made their invasions and committed their murders. One of their leaders, called Peaches, was arrested and induced to lead Crook's troops to the Apache stronghold beyond the border. It was reached and a battle ensued in which the Indians were defeated. A parley ensued, at which the renegades agreed to come back to a reservation selected by themselves on Turkey Creek, near camp Apache. By 1884, these were the most industrious and self-supporting Indians on any reservation.

Chapter XI

WARS WITH OGALLALLAS AND CROWS.

AFTER the Civil war the mountainous country between the Continental divide and the plains came into prominence as a mining section. The rush thither surpassed everthing before known in the northwest. The Alder Gulch region is said to have yielded 50,000,000 of dollars in four years. Helena, Virginia City, Bozeman and other mining towns sprang into existence and were dependent on outside marts for supplies. One route to this new Golconda was by the emigrant road through South Pass and northward by way of Fort Hall. Another, was by boat up the Missouri and Yellowstone and thence through the Crow Indian coutry to the mines. Both of these routes were 500 miles longer than a direct way would have been from Fort Laramie to Bozeman. Preparations for the opening of a direct way—afterwards known as the Montana Road—were begun in 1865, and negotiations for the right to pass through the intermediate Indian countries were opened.

The negotiations would have been easy if the Crows alone had been interested, for almost the entire country was known as "the land of the Crows," of the Dakota family, a nation of tall, well formed hunters and horsemen, who had never been, as a nation, hostile to the whites. But they had been unmercifully punished by the Sioux from the east and north, and had been driven from a great part of their native grounds—known as the Powder River Country, a natural hunting space filled with game of all kinds and therefore very desirable possessions for any Indian tribe.

These facts necessitated treaties for right of way with not only the Crows, who embraced three distinct families, or tribes, but with the Sioux, embracing the families or tribes of Minneconjous, Lower Brules, Two Kettles, Blackfoot Sioux, Sans Arcs, Oncpapas and Ogallallas. The treaties were effected at Fort Sully in October 1865, and they were remarkable, if not suspicious, in the respect that they were signd by very few of the leading Chiefs. The Chiefs who signed for the Ogallallas had no influence with the tribe and their action was repudiated. It was so with many of the others. Even the Crows, natural enemies of the Sioux tribes, could not be held to their treaties.

But it is hardly to be supposed that the government thought these treaties would stand, for simultaneously with their execution it sent General Connor into the Powder River Country to establish Fort Reno, and punish revolting tribes, among whom a powerful anti-treaty sprung up rapidly. This sentiment was most powerful among the three bands of Ogallallas, whose leader was Red Cloud, a warrior of rank and great influence, who professed ability to communicate directly with the Great Spirit, who was his guide in all matters of moment. Red Cloud, as did all the Chiefs of any account, realized that the building of the Montana highway would destroy their favorite hunting grounds and reduce their tribes to a dependent condition. He was ably seconded in his opposition to the treaties by "Man-afraid-of-his-horses," another Ogallalla Chief of great prominence.

The Brule Sioux were, as a tribe, hardly less antagonistic to the treaties than the rest, though their Chief, Spotted-Tail favored them. Spotted-Tail had risen to prominence in his tribe through a love tragedy. He was rival with one of the greatest chiefs for the hand of a comely maiden. The Chief demanded that he should cease his pretensions, as being of no rank in the tribe. Burning with rage, Spotted-Tail snatched his knife and defied his rival. There was a life and death struggle, after which both contestants were found locked in each others arms, seemingly dead. But Spotted-Tail recovered, married his girl, and was elected as Chief of the tribe after the death of the hereditary chief. At the time of the treaties above mentioned his authority was merely nominal, owing to the strong anti-treaty sentiment, though he was counted on by the whites as a sure friend.

Every effort was made to induce the dissenting Indians to come to terms, but they remained undeceived by promises. Military occupation of their country was going on all the time that negotiations were pending. Colonel Carrington was ordered up from Fort Kearney with 2,000 men, of which fully 500 were scattered directly along the route of the proposed new highway. Their presence was a plain menace, and Red Cloud, Man-afraid-of-his-horses, and other chiefs broke off all further negotiations. The Lower Brules with a few stragglers from other tribes were the only Indians who concluded to maintain peace. They numbered at the time 2,500 people, but within a year, Spotted-Tail, Standing Elk and Swift Bear, could not muster over 100 lodges, mostly women and old men, so great had been the defection in their ranks to those of Red Cloud.

The invasion of the Powder River Country went on, in almost entire ignorance of the real sentiment of the Indians. The troops sent were numerous, but poorly equipped for Indian hostilities. On the morning after, a large command reached Fort Reno, 167 miles northwest of Fort Laramie, the very peacefully inclined Sioux ran off all the sutler's horses and mules. They were pursued without effect. Soon after, the troops that had reached Piney Creek were ordered off, with notice that Fort Reno would not be disturbed, but that no other fort could be built in the country. Notwithstanding this notice the foundations of Fort Phil. Kearney were laid on Piney Creek. While at work on this fort, the herd of the builders was stampeded, and the party sent in pursuit was surrounded by Indians and driven back with a loss of two soldiers killed and three wounded. On the same day Indians attacked the trading post of "French Pete," who had married a Sioux wife, and killed the entire party of six men. In the ten days following, five emigrant trains were attacked and fifteen men murdered. A great quantity of stock was run off from under the guns of Fort Reno.

Colonel Carrington now began to find out that the Indians were in earnest, and he sent for re-inforcements. Two companies of regular cavalry were ordered from Fort Laramie and a regiment of infantry from St. Louis. Meanwhile the Indians kept up their depredations, killing emigrants, running off stock, pillaging posts and camps. The building of Fort Phil. Kearney was also going on on an elaborate plan and amid great difficulties. It was inclosed in October, 1866, and was one of the largest forts in the northwest, being 860 feet long by 600 wide, surrounded by a stockade nearly double in size. The proposed new road to Montana crossed the Big Piney just above the fort. Carrington was sent out to build forts and he constructed this one, with his men under constant guard, though he seemingly neglected to ascertain the exact state of things about him by means of trained scouting parties. Some of his best men were captured in the woods and never afterwards heard tell of.

The Indians grew bolder, as soldiers were forced to play carpenter. Now, they attacked the the wood trains, and then rode tantalizingly up to the fort and challenged the soldiers to fight. In November one company of cavalry arrived, and Colonel Fetterman became anxious for a fight. On December 6th, the wood train was attacked two miles from the fort, and forced to corral for defence. Fetterman was sent with a force of infantry and cavalry to attack the Indians and drive them across Lodge Tail Ridge. Carrington went with a small force of mounted infantry back of the Ridge to intercept the Indians on Peno Creek. Fetterman made his attack and routed the Indians whom he pursued for about five miles. They then faced about and returned the attack on Fetterman's troops. His cavalry fled, leaving him with a mere handful of men to face a hundred Indian warriors. Fortunately Carrington's force came up and the Indians retired. Their retreat was a ruse, for Lieutenant Bingham and two or three others who pursued an unmounted Indian for two miles, fell into an ambush and were killed. Red Cloud commanded this Indian force in person. He had a system of watches and signals on the hills, and had, no doubt, prepared this ambuscade for the entire force of whites.

On December 21, 1866, a force of 90 men started into the woods to obtain timber for the fort. At 11 A. M., the look-out was signalled, "Woods full of Indians. Train attacked and coralled. Send relief." Colonel Fetterman was placed in charge of a relief party. Lieutenant Grummond took the cavalry portion in hand. The entire party footed up 84 men. It moved rapidly along the slope of Lodge Trail Ridge and deployed. The Indians abandoned their attack on the wood train, and attacked Fetterman who fought his way over the ridge and into the Valley of Peno Creek. The firing was rapid and continuous, giving evidence at the fort of a hard battle. Colonel Carrington grew anxious, and ordered the men of the wood train to fight their way over the ridge to Fetterman's relief. They tried to do so but were driven back. Another force of 76 men was sent out from the fort under Captain Ten Eyck. It hastened to the ridge to find the firing slacking as though one side were giving way. Looking over the summits of the ridge into Peno Valley it was found to be full of exultant savages who challenged the new comers to attack. Word was sent back to the fort for a howitzer, which did not come. Presently, Ten Eyck noticed that the Indians were withdrawing from the valley on their own account. Venturing down, he found that Fetterman's command had been driven onto a knoll and surrounded. Within a space of about forty feet square lay the bodies of Colonel Fetterman, Captain Brown and 65 men, stripped naked, scalped and mangled beyond description. They had, evidently, been surrounded by greatly superior numbers and shot down at close range. What had become of the rest of the command? Next day a party was sent out to ascertain their fate. A quarter of a mile beyond the pile of dead in the valley was found the dead body of Lieutenant Grummond, and still futher, the bodies of other officers and men, scalped and mutilated as before. The extermination of Fetterman's command had been complete. The victorious Indians were said to number 2,000 warriors made up of various dissatisfied tribes—Ogallallas, Brules, Crows, Arrapahoes, Cheyennes, &c., though the above number is more likely to embrace all who were on the war-path at the time than the number actually engaged in the attack. They reported a loss equal to that of the whites.

This tragedy filled the land with murmurs of rage against the Indians and of disapproval of the military management which had made it possible. General Grant ordered an investigation, the general conclusions of which were that a mighty blunder had been committed but by whom and precisely when and how, nobody could find out. Carrington was removed and was succeeded by General Wessels. About this time Fort Buford, at the mouth of the Yellowstone was attacked by Red Cloud, and the report was that its garrison was massacred entire. But it seemed that one company of cavalry was spared who had beaten off the attack. Wessels tried a winter campaign with no good results. In the spring of 1867, Man-afraid-of-his-horses and other chiefs wanted to reform and join Spotted-Tail's friendly Brules. But as their only excuse was that they wanted powder for hunting, they were not treated with, and hostilities were kept up all summer, the troops on the Montana road having to fight for their wood and water. In August, Major Powells guard was attacked by a large force of Indians and driven in upon his reserve of 30 men stationed behind an improvised fortress made of their iron wagon beds. These troops were well armed with breech-loaders and had plenty of ammunition. They picked off the Indians in such numbers that they drew off and fell back to the hills, where they were joined by Red Cloud's main body, estimated at 1200 warriors. The attack was renewed with determination. For three hours the corral was a blaze of fire and the Indians were swept away by wholesale. The closer they came for attack the more densely they had to mass, and therefore the surer the fire of the besieged. They could stand the withering fire no longer and gave way in flight. Their loss was heavy and they called the battle the "medicine fight," because they thought the whites had supernatural assistance, it being their first taste of medicine administered by the deadly breech-loades. The loss to the whites was but two killed and two wounded.

In the fall of 1867, the Indian Commission decided that the Government had no right to push a road through the Powder River Country. The Pacific Railroad was under way. Army officers and the country were anxious to see it completed. By means of it Montana would be more accessible than by the Bozeman route. The Indians favored it and offered a right of way, if the Government would surrender its claims to the Powder River Country. The treaty of April 29, 1868, was formed, in which the Powder River Country was relinquished to the Indians and a right of way secured for the Pacific Railway. Red Cloud did not sign this treaty till the Government actually began to withdraw its troops from the line of the Montana road. After this was accomplished the various Sioux tribes took possession of the country and demolished the chain of forts which had cost the country such enormous treasure to build and so many precious lives to defend. This treaty, like all others with the Indians, was not destined to stand. A few years later, it was ascertained that the Government had surrendered rights which were too precious and that it would pay to go over the same ground again.

Chapter XII.

THE PIEGAN PUNISHMENT.

THE seats of the Black-Feet tribes were about Lake Winnepeg. Strife among them led to the secession of a large number under the lead of Piegan, or Pheasant, and his name passed to them. Coming south into the territory of the United States, his supporters were augmented by other dissatisfied Black-Feet, Bloods and Gros Ventres, so that they became a formidable tribe.

They are a tall, well formed people with considerable prowess as warriors. Their government is complicated, being composed of seven classes, running down through chiefs, priests. legislators, hunters, warriors, to the lowest ranks. They are sun-worshippers, and the sun dance is the most palpable manifestation of their religious emotion. They have figured in encyclopedias and dime novels as a treacherous, blood-thirsty people, always at enmity with the whites and tireless in their depredations upon them. Much of this is exaggeration. In 1853, they did not hesitate to meet Governor Stevens in council, and his report was that their disposition was undoubtedly friendly. At that time the Bloods and Black-Feet were on Milk River, the Piegans between the Milk and the Missouri, and Gros Ventres on the Missouri below the mouth of Milk River. In 1855 all the tribes of the Upper Missouri, including those mentioned above, met Governor Stevens in council, as had been agreed upon two years before, and not only promised peace among one another but with the United States. A common hunting ground was mapped out, white travellers were to be protected, and the Government was conceded the right to make roads anywhere. Annuities were promised the Indians, and the help of the whites in promoting their civilization.

Ten years of peace passed. The Indians tried agriculture, but the country was too dry. Their annuities were either never paid or were frittered away. There came no promised schools and none of the blessings of civilization. The discovery of gold in the borders of the Blackfoot Country in 1862-1863 attracted thither a mob of white miners who increased the value of their finds by selling whisky to the Indians. In 1864 the Black-Feet offered to help General Sully to whip the Sioux. In the same year the Bloods and trappers were at war, and the Bloods forgot about their treaties and carried their horse stealing to Fort Benton, demolishing the Sun River Agricultural Farm. The enmity of the whites extended to the Piegans, and it was given out that all the Black-Feet nation, except the Gros Ventres, was at war openly or secretly. A militia organization was formed against them, but it never rose above the dignity of a vigilance committee.

In 1866 the restored buildings at Sun River farm were burned, and the arson was blamed on the Piegans, for the reason that they had murdered their Chief, Little Dog, because he had restored some stolen horses to the whites. In 1866-67, these Indians, in common with all others whose living depended on the chase, suffered from want of ammunition and supplies, they having been withheld by the Government on account of the war with the Sioux tribes on the Montana road. Yet there was no outbreak in 1867. In 1868, the white population around Fort Benton began outrages which were well calculated to excite the Indians to war. After the Piegans had signed the treaty of that year, their leader, Mountain Chief, was shot at by two white men, which dastardly act incensed the tribe to revenge, especially after their efforts to have the culprits punished by law failed entirely.

They raided Diamond City and stole 80 horses. Commissioner Cullen seized 18 Piegans and held them till the horses were returned.

The year 1869 showed a worse state of feeling. The Indians revenged themselves on the whites for their lawlessness by stealing their horses and running them over the Canadian borders, where they found ready sale for them. General Sully reported the situation as desperate and said: "Nothing will prevent a general outbreak of the Indians except a sufficient force to clear the country of roughs and whisky sellers."

The Piegans, still smarting under the insult to their Chief, were sympathized with by Red Horn, Bear Chief and others. The depredations, which consisted largely of horse-stealing raids, now turned into mutual surprises and murders, in which whites and reds drew on their devilish ingenuity to the uttermost. Emigrant trains were attacked; ranches were broken up, murders were a matter of almost daily occurrence, and for every murder of a white, two Indians had to pay the penalty with their lives. The Clarke massacre, near Helena, intensified the excitement and seemed to justify a call for the military, but General Sully thought matters would right themselves. In December, a marauding party struck a party of hunters in Sun River valley, and a violent fight ensued. It was resolved to strike back at once, but the great difficulty was to distinguish between friendly and hostile Indians, a matter the settlers had never been very particular about. Indeed it had became a habit to blame every crime on the Piegans and to punish them for every deed committed by roving bands. The camps of Heavy Runner, Big Leg, Little Wolf and The Boy were selected as friendly, and were to remain undisturbed. The camps of Mountain Chief, Bear Chief and Red Horn were to be struck, as hostile.

Colonel Baker left Fort Ellis in January, 1870, with four companies of cavalry. He was re-inforced at Fort Shaw with two companies of mounted infantry, and pushed his way north on the 19th, marching only at night to insure secrecy. On the 23rd, they reached the camp of Bear Chief and Red Horn. Their attack was a complete surprise. Over 300 ponies, their entire herd, was captured, and 173 Indians, including Red Horn, were killed. Only nine Indians escaped, all the rest, men, women and children, fell into the list of killed and captured. Colonel Baker went in search of Mountain Chief's camp, but found only seven deserted lodges on the site. The troops then proceeded to the camps of the Blood chiefs where they demanded all the horses and other property they had stolen. They then returned to their quarters, wearing the laurels of soldiers who had tracked the hostiles to their lair in the dead of winter, surprised a camp stricken with small pox, killed 173 of its occupants, far more than half of whom were women and children.

This attack created great excitement in the East, where it was regarded as a barbarous exhibition of force. The matter found its way into congress and gave rise to many acrimonious debates. Censure was extended clear along the lines up to the commanding officer of the District, and then it took a political turn, some holding Sheridan responsible and others General Hancock.

Though Mountain Chief and perhaps the worst of the Piegan offenders escaped this terrible visitation, they have not proved so troublesome since. Only in 1885 were they reported as dangerously discontented, chiefly because of crop failures and inadequate rations. In nearly all cases the country reserved for these northern tribes is unfit for cultivation. A white man would starve on it. The Indian is expected to change his customs, go to work, and live, where life is impossible. Verily the exactions of the white, the civilized, the christianized peoples are hard. Their code of *meum* and *teum* seems like a wide departure from that divine summary of law " Do unto others as ye would that others should do unto you."

Chapter XIII.

MODOC AND LAVA BED.

THE Modoc tribe are an offshoot of the Klamaths. They occupied the country known as "Lost River Basin," and covering portions of the old Government road to Oregon and California. Their first difficulty was with emigrants, and, according to the Modocs, it grew out of the efforts of the emigrants to recapture horses found in their possession, which they claimed they had purchased from the Snake and Pitt River Indians. Hostilities once begun, continued at intervals, during which time many Modocs were killed and many emigrants were cruelly butchered. Perhaps the most revolting of the many scenes was the massacre of seventy-five whites in 1852. This terrible tragedy called out a company of volunteers for the protection of emigrants. Under the command of Ben. Wright, of Yreka, Cal, they arrived on Tule Lake, at Bloody Point the scene where the seventy-five whites were butchered. They tried to engage the Modocs in a fair battle, but failing in this proposed a "peace talk" which was finally accepted, and forty-six Modoc warriors responded, and were by him and his company attacked and forty-one of them slain. The Modoc people have always remembered this act of treachery which had much to do in perpetuating the bitter feelings that have since existed, and doubtless had influence in the assassination of General Canby and Dr. Thomas. Had Ben Wright been held to account for this unauthorized act, it would have done much to secure the confidence of the Modocs and the tribes as well. But instead of this he was received with great demonstrations, bonfires and banquets, and was afterwards appointed an Indian agent as a reward for this heroic act of treachery to a trusting people, and a violation of the sacred rights of a flag of truce.

Hostilities continued until 1864, when a temporary treaty was made. In the same year, on the 14th of October, Superintendent Huntington of Oregon, under authority of the General Government, held a treaty council at Council Grove, near Fort Klamath, with the Modocs and Klamath Indians, when all the country claimed by these tribes was ceded to the Government, except so much as may be embraced within the boundaries of what is known as Klamath reservation, upon which they agreed and bound themselves to locate immediately after the ratification of treaty. Captain Jack (Kient-poos), and other members of the Modoc tribe signed the treaty in the presence of witnesses. They remained on the reservation several months, accepting goods and subsistence in conformity with the treaty and finally left returning to the Modoc country. They ignored the treaty and refused to return to the reservation until December, 1869. This time they remained on the reservation until April, 1870, and then left for their camp on Lost River. Captain Jack and his band were prepared at this time to remain upon the reservation, and settle down in the way of civilization, if there had been ordinary encouragement and assistance, and if the Klamaths, who largely outnumbered Captain Jack's band, and who were their hereditary enemies, had allowed them to do so. This band began to split rails for their farms, and in other ways to adopt civilized habits; but the Klamaths demanded tribute from them for the land they were occupying, which the Modocs were obliged to render. They also began to taunt the Modocs, calling them "strangers, orphans, poor men," and annoyed them in various ways, claiming the reservation as exclusively their own. Captain Jack appealed to Captain Knapp, the agent, for protection from these insults. At the agent's suggestion they removed to another part of the reservation and began again to try to live by cultivating the ground. But here also they were followed by the same spirit of hostility by the Klamaths, from which they do not seem to have been protected by the agent. The issue of rations seems also to have been suspended for want of funds, and for these reasons Captain Jack and his band returned to their old home on Lost River, where they became a serious annoyance to the whites, who had in the meanwhile settled on their ceded lands.

Renewed petitions for their removal called the attention of Superintendent Odeneal to the subject, who, laying the matter before the Commissioner of Indian Affairs at Washington, was instructed under date of April 1872, to have the Modocs removed to the Klamath reservation and to protect them from the Klamaths. The superintendent sent messengers to the Modoc camp on the 26th of November, 1872, to order them to return to the reservation, and in the event of a refusal on their part to arrange for a meeting with them at Link River, twenty-five miles from the Modoc camp.

They refused compliance with the order, and also refused to meet Superintendent Odeneal, at Link River, saying substantially, "that they did not want to see him or talk with him; that they did not want any white man to tell them what to do; that they intended to remain where they were and would not go to the Klamath reservation; that they were tired of talking and were done talking."

Upon receiving Captain Jack's insolent reply to his message, the superintendent made application to the military commander at Fort Klamath for a force to "compel the Modocs to go upon the Klamath reservation;" giving as an authority the following words from the Commissioner of Indian Affairs:—"You are hereby directed to remove the Modoc Indians to Klamath reservation, peaceably, if you possibly can, but forcibly if you must." He transferred the whole matter to Major John Green commanding the Post, with the hope that he might accomplish the object desired without the shedding of blood, if possible to avoid it.

In compliance with this request Captain Jackson, with about thirty men, left Fort Klamath on November 28th, 1872. They arrived at the Modoc camp on the morning of the 29th and obtained an interview, during which he used every argument in his power to induce them to go. He informed them that ample provision had been made for food and clothing, and that they would be protected from the annoyances of the Klamaths. He also assured them of the folly of resistance to the orders of the Government. Finding his efforts unavailing, he ordered them to "lay down their arms." This order had been partially obeyed and prospects were that no serious trouble would ensue, until the demand was made of "Scar faced Charlie" to surrender, who refused compliance, and Jackson ordered an officer to disarm him. He advanced to perform the duty with pistol drawn, when both the officer and Scar-faced Charlie discharged their arms, but so nearly simultaneously that it is a matter of doubt who fired the first shot. A general engagement then ensued between Jackson's forces and the Modocs in the camp on the west side of Lost River, composed of Captain Jack and some twelve or fifteen other warriors with families. At this point Lost River is a deep stream, three hundred feet wide, dividing the Modoc camp.

While Captain Jack with his band occupied the west bank, ten other warriors with their families occupied the east side. While Jackson's forces were taking position around Captain Jack's Camp, a number of citizens had also taken a position commanding the camp on the east side, and when the former engaged in battle with Captain Jack's band on the west side, the latter soon engaged in battle with those on the east side.

The Modocs kept up the war during the winter, and then retreated into an almost inaccessible volcanic region called the Lava Beds. Here, in the spring of 1873, the Modocs were surrounded but not subdued. In January, 1873, a commission had been appointed by the Secretary of the Interior to inquire into the causes of the difficulties, and to procure, if possible, a peaceable solution of them. This commission, as finally composed, consisted of A. B. Meacham, L. S. Dyar and Rev. Dr. Thomas, and by the direction of the Secretary of the Interior, under date of March 22, 1873, they were put under the direction of General Canby. On the 11th of April, a conference was held with Captain Jack and other representative men of the tribe, but in the midst of the council the treacherous savages rose upon the kind-hearted men who sat beside them, and murdered General Canby and Dr. Thomas in cold blood. Mr. Meacham was also shot and stabbed but escaped with his life. General Canby fell a victim to a bullet from Captain Jack's pistol. Boston Charley first shot Dr. Thomas, and Bogus Charley completed the murder by shooting him with a rifle as he was trying to escape.

When this commission went out from Gillam's camp to meet Capt. Jack, it went warned of possible treachery, and the officers and soldiers were on the alert. As soon as they heard the firing they knew what was up. The soldiers sprang to their arms and ran toward the Council tent. They found the dead bodies of Canby and Dr. Thomas, rescued Meacham, and met Dwyer and Riddle thoroughly exhausted by their efforts to escape. The murderers had fled back into the inaccessible Lava Beds.

This treachery and cruelty made the Modocs objects of universal execration. Extermination of the tribe was now an ultimatum. Gillem's entire command was moved forward in the face of a stubborn resistance and his mortar batteries were trained so that the shells could reach the Indian caves. For two entire days they played on these hiding places, and then the troops advanced to find the Indians had escaped by the rear, through a deep crevice more than a mile in length. The troops had lost six killed and fourteen wounded and the Indians eleven killed.

The Indians took a new position four miles south of their old haunt. Captain Thomas started with a command of 80 men to reconnoitre. While stopping for luncheon, fire was opened on them from the lava ridges around. The men became panic striken and rushed about regardless of orders. Lieutenant Wright reached a ridge on the the west with one company, which was quickly decimated by bullets. Lieutenent Cranston reached a ridge on the north with five men all of whom perished. The main body followed Wright, but they were soon cut down to twenty men. Captain Thomas exclaimed, "We are surrounded, let us die like brave men!" They sheltered themselves as well as they could behind the rocks, but the Indians knew all the by-paths well, and could introduce flank firing without danger to themselves. To add to the horror of the situation, a scout of Warm Spring Indians which came up to the rescue of the troops, was mistaken for Modocs and fired upon by the whites, and their succor was thus prevented. Meanwhile Major Green was hastening to the scene with all the available forces. They reached it in time to save but few of the defeated troops. Captain Thomas, and Lieutenants Howe, Wright and Cranston were dead. Lieutenant Harris was mortally wounded. Eighteen dead and seventeen wounded soldiers were found; the rest of the soldiers gradually struggled back to camp to tell dreadful stories of panic and hair-breadth escapes.

General Jeff. C. Davis succeeded Canby. He found his troops so dispirited over failures and losses as to make a prompt movement unwise. The Modocs inspired fear by keeping quiet. No one knew behind which lava ridge they were crouching, nor what rock might send forth a blast of deadly bullets. At length the Indian scouts reported the capture of a supply train by Modocs, on the east side of Tule Lake. A company of Cavalry was sent after them, which was surprised, but by dint of hard fighting drove off the foe and pursued it back into the Lava Beds.

Davis hit on the plan of forming a number of little camps in the Lava Beds, sufficiently near together to be within supporting distance of one another, and sufficiently numerous to keep the attention of the Indians distracted. If they attempted to surround one, they would be within range of another. Owing to the small number of the Indians this worked great hardship to them. The Modoc Camp, morever, became discordant within. Hooker Jim and Jack quarrelled, and their bands separated, both leaving the Lava Beds. Hooker Jim's party was pursued for fifty miles, the entire way being a series of skirmishes. At length it was run down and forced to surrender. Then Hooker Jim, Bogus Charley, Shack-nasty Jim and Steamboat Frank, volunteered to go as scouts to find Captain Jack and secure his surrender. They found him on Willow Creek, but he would die with his gun in his hand rather than surrender. The troops were following in the direction taken by the scouts, and when informed of the position of Jack's party and of his refusal to surrender, they surrounded him in the Willow Creek Canyon. Boston Charley came out with seven women and surrendered, Jack and the rest of his party escaped by running down the canyon they were pursued over hill and through canyon to the bluffs on Langell's Valley. Here they made a stand, but as the soldiers approached, firing, five Indians rushed forward and surrendered. Jack, with the remaining warriors fled in the night.

There was another hunt after Jack. He was again scented out and surrounded. He now desired to surrender. Coming out of his haunt and glaring about him he said to the scouts "My legs have given out." He was taken to the camp near Clear Lake, where word of his capture was received with joy. One by one the rest of his band was picked up, and the bloody Modoc war came to an end. The loss of life was great measured by the rank and importance of the killed, though in numbers it was not large. Neither was it great on the part of the Indians.

But the war cost the government fully half a million dollars.

General Davis wanted to hang half a score of the surrendered Indians without trial; but the Government ordered a trial by a Military Commission at Fort Klamath. Captain Jack, Schonchin John, Black Jim, Boston Charlie, One-eyed Jim and Slolox were arraigned for murder. Captain Jack made a powerful defence, but there could be but one result. They were all found guilty and sentenced to be hanged. Two of them had their sentences changed to imprisonment for life; the rest were executed at Fort Klamath, October 3, 1873. They were all hanged from one long scaffold, which they mounted firmly and with the assurance that they were "ready to go to the Great Father." The Klamath Indians to the number of 500 witnessed the execution. They had done much to instigate the Modoc uprising, and yet were their chief accusers.

Several of the Modocs, held as prisoners, were murdered. The rest of the tribe was sent east to the Quapaw agency, where their chief, Bogus Charlie, has taught them industry and good behavior. A few of the very worst were sent to Fort Marion, in Florida, and placed in training there. They became converts to Christianity.

Chapter XIV.

CUSTER AND THE SIOUX.

THE Sioux war of 1876 " was dishonorable to the nation, and disgraceful to those who originated it." Such is the language of the Commissioners, appointed to negotiate for the surrender of the Black Hills and unceded Indian country, defined in the treaty of 1868, in their report to the President made on the 18th day of December, 1876.

By the treaty of 1868, it will be remembered, there was set apart for the absolute and undisturbed use of the Sioux, for their permanent home, all that part of Dakota lying south of parallel 46 and east of the Missouri River, together with the reservations on the east side of the Missouri and the country lying north of the North Platte River and east of the summit of the Big Horn Mountains. According to the terms of the treaty this reservation " is set apart for the absolute and undisturbed use and occupation of the Indians herein named and for such other friendly tribes or individual Indians as from time to time they may be willing, with the consent of the United States, to admit amongst them; and the United States now solemnly agrees that no persons, except those therein designated and authorized so to do, and except such officers, agents and employees of the Government as may be authorized to enter upon Indian reservations in discharge of duties enjoined by law, shall ever be permitted to pass over, settle upon, or reside in the territory described in this article, or in such territory as may be added to this reservation for the use of said Indians." Another article provides, "that the country north of the North Platte and east of the Big Horn Mountains, shall be held and considered unceded Indian territory, and the United States also stipulates and agrees that no white person or persons shall be permitted to settle upon or occupy any portion of the same, or without the consent of the Indians first had and obtained, to pass through the same." The Indians on their part agree "to relinquish all right permanently to occupy the territory outside of their reservation as defined in the treaty, but yet reserve the right to hunt on any lands north of the North Platte, and on the Republican fork of the Smoky Hill River." The United States also agreed to abandon the Montana road with all the forts along it. It was left

RED CLOUD.

to the Indians to choose whether they would be farmers or hunters. To the farmers, however, a larger annuity would be given. Owing to lack of rain, abundance of grasshoppers, and their own inclination, many of them naturally continued to follow the chase.

In less than three months after this treaty was ratified and proclaimed, it was violated by the government. On June 20th, 1869, General Sheridan, by order of General Sherman, issued the following military order: "All Indians, when on their proper reservations, are under the exclusive control and jurisdiction of their agents; they will not be interfered with in any manner by the military authority, except upon requisition of the special agent resident with them, his superintendent, or the bureau of Indian Affairs at Washington. Outside the well defined limits of their reservations, they are under the original and exclusive authority of the military, and as a rule will be considered hostile."

Though this order was in direct violation of certain provisions of the treaty of 1868, granting the privilege of roaming and hunting on the unceded Indian country, yet it was inexorably executed, the Indians were attacked and punished whenever they could be found by the military. The Indians could not understand why they should be thus hunted, harassed and punished by the soldiers, since they were only exercising a right secured to them by the treaty, especially as they still continued to receive the annuity granted to the Indians that *hunted and roamed.* While the Sioux were punished for not obeying a military order, given in violation of the treaty, the whites were making constant incursions upon their territory.

When the treaty was made in 1868, the country set apart for the Indians was supposed to be in a large part of waste and barren land. But between 1868 and 1876, when war was declared against the Sioux, many and great changes had taken place. These changes were due to the settling of the new country, adjacent to the Indian reservations, opened up by the North Pacific Railroad and numerous minor lines, and the "Black Hills" gold fever. Great numbers of these settlers began to look with longing eyes towards the Black Hills, which by the treaty of 1868 was declared to be an inviolable part of the Sioux reservation. Indians, from time to time, brought in gold dust and nuggets to the trading posts. When questioned, they admitted that they found it in the Black Hills. The story spread like wild-fire and the excitement waxed high in the west. Parties of miners began to organize for the new Eldorado and the government was petitioned to sanction this trespass. Notwithstanding the protests of the Indians, numerous expeditions under the escort and protection of the Military were made into the Black Hills and other parts of their reservation. But what incensed the Sioux most was the formidable expedition fitted out under General Custer in the Summer of 1874. This strong column was formed with the avowed purpose of ascertaining whether gold was to be found there. It consisted of ten companies of the Seventh Cavalry, Company I, Twentieth Infantry and Company G, Seventeenth Infantry, with sixty Indian scouts and four Gatling guns. General Forsyth was with the column.

There was little or no danger to the powerful column either real or apprehended. It started on a romantic and mysterious expedition, as if for a picnic, and as such it found the whole journey. When Custer applied for Indian scouts, who were Sioux, to accompany the expedition they were very much surprised. They hesitated and expressed regret, but could not do otherwise than obey the summons. Custer's reports of the progress of this expedition was given in such glowing terms that those who heard grew wild with excitement. "Not only was there gold to be found, but the country was beautiful beyond description and not the barren waste heretofore supposed.

The next morning, although loath to leave so enchanting a locality, we continued to ascend this valley until gradually, almost imperceptibly, we discovered that we were on the crest of the western ridge of the Black Hills; and instead of being among barren, rocky peaks, as might be supposed, we found ourselves wending our way through a little park, whose natural beauty may well bear comparison with the loveliest portions of Central Park. Favored as we had been in having Floral Valley for our roadway to the west of the Black Hills, we were scarcely less fortunate in the valley, which seemed to me to meet us on the interior slope."

This expedition remained out until September, and further explorations only confirmed Custer's first impressions. Upon its return a full report was given in which the people were told that it was a "goodly land," beautiful to look upon, abounding in good water, timber and grass. Yes, and gold was to be found there. It was this confirmation of former reports that kept the covetous eyes of the whites turned towards the Black Hills, and more mining parties were organized and started for them. The Northern Pacific Railroad,

STANDING HOLLY. (Sitting Bull's Daughter.)

too, changed its line from the north to the south side of the Yellowstone river

This change was very objectionable to the nomad Sioux, they claiming that it was in violation of the treaty of 1868, and that it frightened away the buffalo. They therefore drove off the surveying parties who attempted to run this new line. Numerous depredations were committed upon the Indians by the white rowdies, horse-theives, and scalawags, who congregate in a new and lawless country. They also preyed upon the white settlers, and most of this was credited to the Indians. Stock was taken from the Indians and by the Indians. Blood was shed on both sides. The Indians were branded as "fiends" while the outlaws who preyed upon both white and Indians were termed the "pioneers of the frontier." All this was not calculated to soothe the savage breast and make it tender and loving toward the white man.

Some officers who did not accompany the Custer expedition characterized his report as baseless and exaggerated. General Hazen designated all that part of the Northwest as a "Barren Belt." A dispute also arose among the geologists, as to the mining value of the Black Hills. Another expedition was therefore sent out in the Summer of 1875, under Professor

Jenney, with a military escort under Lieutenant Colonel Dodge. They entered Floral Valley a month earlier than Custer had, and were greeted by a violent storm of sleet, but later on found both soil and climate congenial. They also found the country full of miners, contrary to the treaty stipulations. General Crook was instructed to order them to leave.

A month later, on August 10, 1875, Red Cloud said to Governor Fletcher, of Missouri, who was at the Red Cloud agency: "Now as to those Black Hills, Our Great Father has got a great many soldiers, and I never knew him, when he wanted to stop anything with his soldiers, but he succeeded in it. The reason I tell you this, is that the people from the states who have gone to the Black Hills, are stealing our gold, digging it out and taking it away, and I don't see why the Great Father don't bring them back. To this the Governor replied:—"The Great Father has ordered these people away from there in five days from now, and if they do not go, he will bring them out with his soldiers." On the next day, Sitting Bull said:—"You told me yesterday that the troops would take all the white people away from the Black Hills by the 15th of August, and the young men were all very glad to know that these miners were to be out of the Black Hills before the Northern Indians came down to the grand council." In reply to Sitting Bull, Governor Fletcher said :—"I saw General Crook, and he said he had orders from the President to get these miners all out by the 15th of this month, and the miners have all agreed to go by that time."

General Crook went to the hills and advised the miners to leave. Some did so in good faith, others went away to return again, still others doggedly remained. General Crook reported that he had given them time to secure themselves against loss, but that the sentiment was strong against removal. They charged that the Indians violated the treaties every year by their predatory incursions. He advised that steps be taken to secure a cession of the mining regions from the Indians. If this was not done there would surely be trouble when the miners attempted to return.

In Nov. 1875, E. C. Watkins, Indian Commissioner, reported that the "Sioux country is probably the best hunting ground in the United States, a paradise for Indians, affording game in such variety and abundance that the need of government supplies is not felt. Perhaps for this reason they have never accepted aid or been brought under control. They openly set at defiance all law and authority, and boast that the

United States are not strong enough to conquer them. The troops are held in contempt, and, surrounded by their native mountains, relying on their knowledge of the country and powerful endurance, they laugh at the futile efforts that have thus far been made to subjugate them, and scorn the idea of white civilization. They are lofty and independent in their attitude and language toward the government officials, as well as the whites generally, and claim to be the sovereign rulers of the land. They say they own the wood, the water, the ground, the air, and that white men live in or pass through their country but by their sufferance. They are rich in horses and robes, and are thoroughly armed. Nearly every warrior carries a breech loading gun, a pistol, a bow, and a quiver of arrows. Inspector Watkins did not seem to be familiar with the terms of the treaty of 1868, by which these wild bands of Sioux had the right guaranteed to them to roam and hunt in the valleys where they then were, and in all other parts of the unceded Indian country, as long as game abounded.

In December, 1875, the Secretary of the Interior ordered the Sioux to remove to a reservation on penalty of being reported to the War Department as hostiles. This order was sent to the agents of the respective tribes, to be commun-

SIOUX ON THE WARPATH.

icated to Sitting Bull and other wild Indians. This order was to take effect in January, 1876. These wild Indians were nomads, roaming and hunting on unceded lands by virtue of the treaty of 1868. Some of the Indians acquiesced in the order, others knew that there was not food enough for them at the agencies, and so declined to come till they had supplied themselves with buffalo meat, still others never heard of the order. Sitting Bull sent word that he would not comply. Very many of the agency Indians were out hunting. These were disarmed as they returned. When this became known the hunting parties still out refused to return, but joined the forces of Sitting Bull.

Sitting Bull's declination was anticipated, and he and his followers were turned over to the tender mercy of the War Department. An expedition was speedily dispatched against them, in which the miners were a unit with the troops, for it was clear that the Black Hills region must be wrested from the Indians.

The war, aptly styled "the crime of the centennial year," was therefore begun against the Sioux. Three colums of troops were ordered to concentrate on the upper waters of the Yellowstone. General Terry started from Fort Lincoln with one column, 1,000 strong, in which was

Custer's command. General Crook had command of the Fort Fetterman column, 1,300 men. General Gibbon led the one from Fort Ellis, with 400 men. Crook reached the field first and sent General Reynolds to look up the band of Crazy Horse, then encamped near Bear Butte, and detained there by the cold weather. On March 17, 1876, Reynolds surprised this camp, capturing 800 ponies, and destroying the teepes and goods. The Indians rallied on the mountain sides and made a determined stand, pouring in a destructive fire on the troops. The troops were re-inforced and finally succeeded in beating the Indians off, so that a retreat could be effected. This retreat was kept up for 20 miles, during which the whites lost most of the captured ponies. In this engagement the Indians were surprised but by no means beaten. Crook returned to Fort Fetterman, on account of the cold. where he remained till May 29th.

This expedition gave rise to the impression that the hostile Sioux were not so numerous as had been supposed. This false impression became the basis of future forces and movements. How fatal it was, we shall soon see. Crook opened his summer campaign by marching from For Fetterman to Fort Reno. By June 8th he was on Tongue River, where he was joined by a number of Crow, Shoshone and Nez Perces Indians as scouts. The camps of Sitting Bull and Crazy Horse were reported to be on the Rosebud River. Thither Crook marched expecting to surprise the camp. But he was suddenly attacked by Sitting Bull, and the "Battle of the Rosebud" was fought June 17th, 1876. Crook deployed to a disadvantage owing to the contour of the ground. Sitting Bull handled his forces with great skill, taking advantage of every defect in Crook's lines. The ground was hotly contested, and the white troops were forced into a retreat, which for a time foreboded disaster. But they were reformed and pushed the battle with great gallantry, finally holding the field, but unable to pursue and punish.

The two colums of Terry and Gibbon had communicated with each other near the junction of the Tongue and Yellowstone Rivers. The Indians were found to be in force beyond the Yellowstone, and Terry began to feel for them along the lines of the Powder, Tongue, Rosebud, Little and Big Horn Rivers. Major Reno was sent with six companies of the 7th Cavalry to the Powder River with orders to communicate with Crook. He found neither Crook nor Indians. Both the Tongue and Powder Rivers were declared to be free from Indians. The search narrowed to the Rosebud and Big and Little Horn Rivers. As soon as Terry received Reno's report he ordered General Custer to march to a point south of Gibbon, on the Yellowstone. Terry kept abreast of his column, on the little steamer Far West. When Gibbon's camp was reached, a consultation was held. It was believed the Indians were on the Rosebud or Little or Big Horn and Terry announced that General Custer should strike them a blow.

Custer started up the Rosebud on June 22nd, with orders to proceed south to the head-waters of the Tongue, and then turn toward the Little Big Horn, but leaving him unhampered should occasion require. Colonel Gibbon's column was already in motion toward the mouth of the Big Horn, intending to cross and move to the parks of the Big and Little Big Horn. Custer and Gibbon were to communicate as often as possible.

Custer marched his regiment twelve miles up the Rosebud on June 22nd. On the 23rd and 24th he continued his march, following an Indian trail, which freshened every mile. He then halted to await his scouts. The report came that the Indian camp seemed to be on the Little Big Horn. To reach it the divide between the Rosebud and the Little Big Horn would have to be crossed, and in order to do this in safety the march would

Frank Gates. Short Bull. Charles P. Gordon. Feathers-on-his-head. Fire Thunder. Mrs. Black Bull Bear.

A GROUP OF SIOUX CHIEFS.

have to be at night. The movement began at 11 P. M., of the 24th, and the column filed up a branch of the Rosebud, which headed near the summit of the divide. The scouts brought word that the divide could not be crossed except in daylight. A halt was called; breakfast was taken. At 8 A. M. of the 25th the divide was crossed and the column began to descend a branch of the Little Big Horn. Indians had been seen and a surprise was now out of the question. It was determined to move in direct attack. Custer kept command of Companies C, E, F, I and L. Reno commanded Companies M, A and G. Benteen commanded Companies H, D and K. McDougall held Company B as a guard for the train. Reno moved to the left; Benteen further to the left. Custer kept to the right of the creek. In this order the forces moved down toward the Little Big Horn and the valley. By 12.30 P. M., the village was reported as only two miles ahead and running away. Reno was ordered to push forward as fast as possible, and he would be supported by all the rest. He quicked marched for two miles to a fording, stopped to gather his battalions, and sent hasty word to Custer that the enemy was in force before him, and strong. He deployed and charged down the valley, driving the Indians for over two miles with great ease.

Fearing a trap and not finding the support Custer had promised, yet not wishing to retreat, though the Indians began to swarm around him, he dismounted his men, and took possession of a point of wood for defence He soon found he was fighting odds five to one, and that he must get out of the woods to escape being surrounded and captured. He remounted his men and charged on the Indians between him and the bluffs on the opposite side of the river. This desperate charge cost him the lives of 3 officers and 29 men.

He gained the bluffs, however, and was met by Benteen's three companies, which raised his force to 380 men. Hearing nothing of Custer, and thus reinforced, he moved along the bluffs toward the Indian camp again. Firing was heard off in the direction of the village. The supposition was it was Custer, and an effort was made to communicate with him, which failed. Reno then returned to his first position on the bluffs, dismounted his men, sheltered their horses in a depression, and had hardly done so when he was furiously attacked. The attack lasted till 9 P. M., and occasioned a loss of 18 killed and 46 wounded.

Reno was now impressed with the fact that the overwhelming force of the enemy would prevent Custer from coming to his support. He therefore dug rifle pits and prepared barricades of dead horses and mules, so as to be prepared for the next day. All night his men worked within sound of a scalp-dance-in the valley below. At half past two in the morning his positon suddenly became the centre of a terrific fusilade, which increased till daylight. Reno found himself completely surrounded by swarms of daring savages, who boldly charged his lines at 9 A. M., but were repulsed. On the morning of the 27th, troops were seen coming to their relief. Where was Custer all this time? Of all his command there was only one left to tell, Curly, the Crow Indian Scout. His story runs:

Custer, with his five companies, after separating from Reno and his seven companies, moved to the right around the base of a high hill overlooking the valley of the Little Horn. There were no signs of Indians in the hills on that side (the right) of the Little Horn, and the column moved steadily on until it rounded the hill and came in sight of the village lying in the valley below them. Custer appeared very much elated, and ordered the bugles to sound a charge, and moved on at the head of his column, waving his hat to encourage his men. When they neared the river, the Indians, concealed in the undergrowth on the opposite side of the stream, opened fire on the troops, which checked the advance. Here a portion of the command were dismounted and thrown forward to the river, and returned the fire of the Indians. During this time the warriors were seen riding out of the village by hundreds, and deploying across Custer's front and to his left, while the women and children were seen hastening out of the village in large numbers in the opposite direction. During the fight at this point, Curly saw two of Custer's men killed, who fell into the stream. After fighting a few moments here, Custer seemed to be convinced that it was impracticable to cross, as it only could be done in column of fours, exposed during the movement to a heavy fire from the front and both flanks. He therefore ordered the head of the column to the left, and bore diagonally into the hills, down stream, his men on foot leading their horses.

In the meantime the Indians had crossed the river (below) in immense numbers, and began to appear on his right flank and in his rear; and he had proceeded but a few hundred yards in the new direction the column had taken, when it became necessary to renew the fight with the Indians who had crossed the stream. At first the command remained together, but after some minutes fighting it was divided, a portion deploying circularly to the left, and the remainder similarly to the right, so that when the line was formed, it bore a rude resemblance to a circle, advantage being taken, as far as possible, of the protection afforded by the ground. The horses were in the rear, the men on the line being dismounted, fighting on foot. Of the incidents of the fight in other parts of the field than his own, Curly was not well-informed, as he was himself concealed in a deep ravine, from which but a small part of the field was visible.

The fight appeared to have begun, about 2.30 or 3 o'clock P. M., on the 25th, and continued without intermission until nearly sunset. The Indians had completely surrounded the command, leaving their horses in ravines well to the rear, themselves pressing forward to the attack on foot. Confident in the great superiority of their numbers, they made several charges on all points of Custer's lines, but the troops held their position firmly, and delivered a heavy fire, which every time drove them back. The firing was a continuous roll, or, as he expressed it, "like the snapping of threads in the tearing of a blanket." The troops expended all the ammunition in their belts, and then sought their horses for the reserve ammunition carried in their saddle pockets.

As long as their ammunition held out, the troops, though losing considerably in the fight, maintained their position in spite of all the efforts of the Sioux. From the weakening of their fire toward the close of the afternoon, the Indians appeared to believe that their ammunition was about exhausted, and they made a grand final charge, in the course of which the last of the command was destroyed, the men being shot where they lay in their positions in the line, at such close quarters that many were killed with arrows. Curly said that Custer remained alive throughout the greater part of the engagement, animating his men to determine resistance, but about an hour before the close of the fight he received a mortal wound.

The Crow said, further, that the field was thickly strewn with the dead bodies of the Sioux, who fell in the attack—in numbers considerably more than the force of soldiers engaged. He was satisfied that their loss exceeded 200 killed, besides an immense number wounded. Curly accomplished his escape by drawing his blanket around him in the manner of the Sioux, and passing through an interval which had been made in their lines as they scattered over the field in their final charge.

In most particulars the account given by Curly of the fight is confirmed by the position of the trail made by Custer in his movements and the general evidences of the battle field. The famous Sioux chief, Gall, who had an important command among the hostiles during the battle, on being taken over the field in 1888, by the officers at Fort Custer, confirmed the statement of the Crow scout. Custer, according to Gall, did not succeed in crossing the river.

He saw at a glance that he was overpowered, and did the only thing proper under the circumstances, in leading his command to higher ground where it could defend itself to some advantage. Even in that dread extremity, his soldier spirit and noble bearing held the men under control, and the dead bodies of the troopers of Calhoun's and Keough's companies, found by General Gibbon's command lying in ranks as they fell, attested the cool generalship exhibited by the heroic leader in the midst of deadly peril. It had always been General Custer's habit to divide his command when attacking Indian villages. His victory over Black Kettle on the Washita was obtained in that manner, but the experiment proved fatal to Major Elliott, and a considerable squad of soldiers. It was the general opinion in Crook's command at the time, that had an officer of more resolution been in Major Reno's place, he would have attempted to join Custer at any cost. Reno was, no doubt, imposed upon by Indian strategy, and his retreat to the bluffs, was to say the least of it, premature. But, in the light of after events, it does not seem probable that he could have reached the fatal heights upon which Custer and his men perished. Had Custer taken his entire regiment into the fight he might still have sustained a repulse, but would have escaped annihilation.

Meanwhile Gibbon had pushed his command forward so that he could reach the Little Big Horn by scouts. On the morning of the 26th, three Crow scouts brought him word of Custer's massacre. Gibbon then entered the valley of Little Big Horn with his whole Infantry force. The enemy retreated, and Gibbon forced his men ahead till he reached the fortified position held by Reno. The rescue was a welcome one, for Reno was holding on with sheer desperation and was liable to Custer's fate at any moment. The Indians quailed before the advent of Gibbon's command and took to the mountains, burning all they could not carry.

Gibbon started to find Custer. A march of a few miles brought him upon the field of blood. The sight that met his eyes was shocking in the extreme. Over those bluffs, naked and mutilated, were thickly strewn the dead bodies of Custer's men. Near the summit, they found the body of the gallant Custer. Gibbon's regiment buried the dead on the field where they fell. After the dead were buried, Generals Terry and Gibbon slowly and sadly retraced their way to Rosebud Landing, on the Yellowstone, where, like Crook, they awaited re-inforcements.

The Indians now divided. Sitting Bull kept the Valley of Long Fork, while Crazy Horse moved eastward. Re-inforcements were hurried to the seat of war. Crook scouted Tongue River, and started for the Black Hills. General McKenzie moved in October upon the Red Cloud Agency and siezed the arms and ponies belonging to Red Cloud's band. This was white savagery in the extreme, yet war seemed to justify it by the fact that so many of the agency Indians were deserting, with their arms, to the hostiles.

It was in October, 1876, that General Miles was met by Sitting Bull with propositions for peace. He would listen to no terms that deprived him of his right to live as a free Indian. The dissolution of the Council meant that hostilities would be renewed. Both sides took position and a battle ensued in which the Indians were routed and chased for forty miles. 400 lodges surrendered, and 119 gained the Yankton reservation, where they dissolved. Sitting Bull escaped to the north.

A new expedition was fitted out by General Crook, and on the 7th of December, Lieutenant Baldwin attacked Sitting Bull and drove him across the Missouri. On the 18th he surprised their camp, capturing all its contents. In a state of destitution, Sitting Bull's band escaped across the Yellowstone where he received word from Crazy Horse to join his camp.

This was prevented by General Miles. Crazy Horse was driven from his winter camp on the Tongue River, and followed until on the morning of Jan. 8th, a fight ensued between Miles' force and 600 braves, in which the Indians were repulsed with heavy loss and driven back over the Wolf Mountains whence they fled to the Big Horn range. Here Miles sent word to them that they must surrender. This they concluded to do. On May 6th, 889 people and 2,000 ponies under Crazy Horse, came into Camp Robinson and surrendered to General Crook. Sitting Bull and the remnant of his little band fled across the Canada line where he was joined by other Chiefs. On the 20th day of July 1881, Sitting Bull returned with all that was left of his once powerful camp, and surrendered at Fort Buford.

Chapter XV.

THE NEZ PERCES WARS.

IN these pages the reader has already become acquainted with the Nez Perces, and has learned that they have, as a rule, been friendly. Their friendship has been sorely tested at times, both by their surroundings and by the folly of the whites, but it has ever proved of good quality. They invited missionaries in early times, they shared the patriotic enmity of our settlers against the encroachments of England, when her Hudson Bay Company would have stolen the whole of the North-west territory, they offered protection to the Lapwai mission after Whitman had fallen at Wailatpu, they stood for peace during the disturbances of 1855. While they may not have been forward in adopting the civilization of the white man, they have always proved a friend.

They are racially, upper and lower Nez Perces. Of the latter, Joseph was chief, when Whitman was massacred. He came to meet the Oregon Volunteers with the speech:—"When I left home

I took the Book in my hand and brought it with me. It is my light. I heard the Americans were coming to kill me. Still I held my Book before me and came on."

The Nez Perces never had a central chief of their own choosing. The Upper and Lower nations conceded the right of visitation, hunting and fishing to each other, but as to the control of their lands, the right was in the tribe which occupied them permanently.

The Nez Perces occupied desirable seats, so far as their tastes went. The Lower Nez Perces were bounded on one side by the Snake River, and on the other by the Blue Mountains. Between are mountains and valleys, in such rapid succession as to make the country undesirable for whites, yet loveable to the Indians. Their Chief Joseph was an astute philosopher, with notions of land tenure that astonished those who came to treat with him and with a care for his people that was patriarchal. He would not sell land because no man owned any part of the earth. It was God's gift to all, and for a man to assume to part with what was not his own was impious. He refused to ratify the treaty of 1859, and advised his people not to receive the money and presents offered by the Government, lest the white man should say he had bought what the Indian could not sell.

By 1863 the encroachment of the whites on the Nez Perces was such, and the quality of the whisky sold them was so bad, that conflicts arose and another treaty, as a means of further cheating them, was deemed necessary. By this treaty the Upper Nez Perces agreed to accept the limits of the reservation mapped for them at Lapwai. The Lower Nez Perces refused to join in the treaty. But that did not save their lands for them.

The Upper Nez Perces sold all their lands, not set forth in their reservation. This sale, by judicial knavery known only where English is spoken, was made to comprehend the lands of the Lower Nez Perces. The logic was that inasmuch as Joseph had joined the other chiefs in giving title to lands sold as far back as 1855, he thereby acknowledged the tribal relation of the Nez Perces. Therefore, when the Northern Nez Perces chose to sell lands, they necessarily sold tribal lands, that is they sold Joseph's lands, or the lands of the Lower Nez Perces. This trick of law and travesty on justice was an afterthought on the part of the authorities, for Joseph died in 1871, in blissful ignorance of the fact that his tribe had no place in which to subsist.

Joseph was succeeded by his son, Thunder-travelling-over-the-Mountains. He was the younger Joseph of the Nez Perces, six feet tall, grave and cautious, exact and resolute. He and his brother Ollacut were educated in Mrs. Spalding's Mission School. Though the whites continued to swarm in his country, he ruled so as to avoid war. Even when outrages on Indians began in 1871, he took no revenge, but never abated his argument that the white man should leave the country.

In 1875 and 1876, the conduct of the whites became unbearable. Indians were killed in sprees and quarrels, and yet no murder could be indicted. Joseph relied on that broken reed—the law, but it never came to vindicate the wronged of his tribe. In 1873 the question of title to the lands of the Lower Nez Perces reached a crisis. It was not thought that the sale made of outside lands by the Upper Nez Perces included those of the Lower Nez Perces. So steps were taken to set the Wallowa section off as a reservation for the Lower Nez Perces. Congress refused to confirm the steps, for the reasons given above. The lands had already been sold and the Lower Nez Perces would have to go on the Lapwai reservation with their northern brothers.

The consummation of this outrage excited the attention of many people in Oregon who had not forgotten the good services of the Nez Perces in the past. They interested themselves in the formation of a commission to investigate the matter. General O. O. Howard, then commanding the District of Columbia, was made a member of the Commission. The Commission met at Lapwai and had long talks with the Chiefs. Joseph quite non-plussed them with the wisdom and truth of his statements. But marvelous as it may seem, though there was no attempt to counteract his wisdom, or dispute his facts, this Commission chosen in a christian spirit and for the purpose of meting justice, ratified the sale of Joseph's lands without his consent, and decided that if the Lower Nez Perces did not leave their country and go on to the Lapwai reservation they should be driven there by force. The same Commission recommended that the Cayuses, Umatillas and Walla-Walla's vacate their peaceful homes and go on to the Umatilla reservation, because their numbers were too small to hold such quantities of land when so many white agriculturists were waiting to occupy them.

General Howard was the agent to enforce the decision of the Commission, by virtue of his office. He held several councils, which were of no avail, except in that it was made plain that the Indians must go on to the Lapwai reservation or fight. Joseph decided not to fight, but he could not control all his chiefs. Too-hul-hul-sute counseled resistance, and Joseph's decision was overruled. They formed war parties, armed themselves thoroughly, practiced infantry and cavalry tactics. When the 30 days given them to vacate were up they were in excitement ready to resist. Their young bucks could not be restrained, and they engaged in murderous excesses. Blood whetted their appetites and they rode to camps showing the scalps they had taken. Joseph and Ollacut remained unmoved, but White Bird gave way and joined the riotous throng. Twenty warriors rode out of camp and back to Salmon River. Each one had his spite against some settler who had wronged him, and his hour for revenge had come. Several murders were committed and many houses were burned. These excesses were only drawing on them a sorry fate. They made war inevitable, but not until it became so did Joseph cease his advice for peace. Then he took command, and moved his forces to White Bird Canyon.

Colonel Perry came up in haste from Fort Lapwai, with 90 men. He entered the canyon, across which Joseph had stretched his men, hidden by bushes and rocks. He had also ambushed a party of cavalry behind a hill on the south of the canyon. When the soldiers came within range every bush and rock poured out its concealed fire. At the same moment the mounted warriors appeared on the left. Perry deployed his force so as to meet both attacks. Men were falling thick and fast. The cry of "fall back to the next ridge" was heard. The troops fell back, but the enemy were on their heels. The troops were in confusion. They could not stop at the ridge and all efforts to rally them proved unsuccessful. The Indians were pressing in on all sides to sunder the column and cut off retreat. Captain Teller was cut off, and wheeled into a side ravine, only to have his command cut to pieces. A few only struggled up the steep sides and made their escape. The troops were now in full retreat, and were pursued for twelve miles. Sixty-five of them made their escape and re-formed far from the scene of battle and defeat. The quiet, unostentatious, friendly nation of Indians was in a twinkling transformed into doughty warriors, whose conquest would require heavy reinforcements.

Additional troops were sent from all points. Skirmishing became almost continuous. The camp of Looking Glass, a friendly, was attacked and destroyed, but his warriors escaped to Joseph. Lieutenant Rains and ten men went on a scout. The entire force was killed. General Howard came up with all the troops he could muster—400 fighting men, with gatling guns and a howitzer. Joseph had crossed to the Clear Water with 300 warriors. Here battle was joined. The troops had left their supply trains ungarded. Joseph saw this and sent 30 warriors to capture it. They were driven off by the cavalry, who detected the move in the nick of time. All afternoon the main battle progressed. Charges and counter-charges were made with varying effects. All night both sides strengthened their positions and kept up the firing. In the morning fierce battle was renewed and continued till noon. Howard received a re-inforcement of cavalry, which joined the artillery in a charge on the Indians left. The fighting was furious for some time, but the Indians recoiled, broke and fled across the Clear Water, where they re-formed in sufficient numbers to protect the flight of the rest.

They were pursued by the troops, the next morning, but the pursuing column was ambushed by the rear guard of the Nez Perces and thrown into confusion. Night found the Indians strongly encamped at the entrance to Solo trail. Joseph's second battle had not been a victory but he had conducted a masterly retreat. It was designed to trap Joseph in this long and tortuous trail. But he was too wary for the troops. He threaded its mazes to the valley of the Lou-Lou, and thence to the Bitter Root. General Gibbon, with a force of 190 cavalry from Helena, tried to intercept them on the Bitter Root, but failed. They had gone into the valley of the Big Hole River. Here they thought they were secure, but Gibbon had followed them closely and caught up with them. In the dim light of early morning he struck their camp and charged completely through it. The surprise seemed complete, but the warriors rallied and retook their camp. They drove the troops back behind defences and kept up battle with them through the day. Gibbon fell, wounded, and his howitzer fell a prize to the enemy. At night the Indians retreated leaving the troops so badly used up that they could not follow. The third battle was Joseph's victory. It was here that Howard joined Gibbon, and where the humane generals of the white troops permitted their Bannock auxiliaries to scalp the dead Nez Perces braves. The Nez Perces took no scalps and never mutilated the slain. Their greatest loss in this battle was their ablest diplomat, Looking Glass.

Joseph now crossed the divide into Idaho and camped on the Camas prairie. He was pursued by Howard, who also encamped on the prairie. Joseph planned a surprise, by which he ran off a great number of Howard's horses. Leaving his pursuer crippled, he passed through Tacker's Pass into the Yellowstone Park, down the Yellowstone Lake, over the river through Clark's Canyon and back to the Yellowstone again. This feint was to avoid Sturgis' command of 350 cavalry, who thought to head Joseph off in the valley of the Stinking Water River. But Sturgis soon found he had been deceived, and took up the chase in the right direction. He struck the rear guard of the Nez Perces beyond the Yellowstone, and, though met by a severe fire, he pressed it so closely as to capture 400 ponies. The Indians entered Canyon Creek where they repelled attack throughout the day. In the morning Sturgis received a large re-inforcement of Crow Indians, who succeeded in capturing 500 more ponies from the Nez Perces. Joseph then retreated up the Mussel Shell River, back of Judith Mountain, and struck the Missouri at Cow Island, 123 miles below Fort Benton. Here they attacked the guards and burned the goods at the landing. A force from Fort Benton came down to attack them, but gave up in despair after a skirmish or two.

The Indians moved slowly northward and encamped near the British line on Snake Creek. The telegraph was fleeter than their ponies. Colonel Miles had left Fort Keogh with a large force of infantry, cavalry and a deadly Hotchkiss. Joseph did not know of this new force, which struck his trail at Cow Island. He was resting in his camp, when it was suddenly attacked and a herd of 800 cattle cut off. Two battalions of cavalry charged upon his camp, but were repulsed with the loss of a fifth of their force. Miles then disposed his forces so as to surround the Indians. The whites had the best of the situation but dare not attack, except at long range with shells from the howitzer. For four days this situation was maintained. The Indians could have escaped at any time, if they had agreed to leave behind their wounded, and the women and children. But this says Joseph, "We were unwilling to do. We never heard of a wounded Indian getting well while in the hands of a white man."

Joseph had hope that Sitting Bull would come from his camp over the British line to his rescue. To this end, he waited and parlied with General Miles for several days. At length he concluded to surrender all that was left of his band. Ollacut, Dreamer-Drummer, Too-hul-hul-sute, and 27 others had perished here at this last camp. White Bird had made his escape with 105 warriors, and had crossed into Canada. Joseph made most honorable terms. He well knew he would have to go on to a reservation, but he got the trip postponed till the pleasant weather of Spring, and was not deprived of any of his cattle or effects.

Of this war General Sherman says:—

"Thus terminated one of the most extraordinary Indian wars on record. The Indians throughout displayed a courage and skill that elicited universal praise. They abstained from scalping, let captive women free, did not murder peaceful families and fought with almost scientific skill, using rear guards, skirmish lines and field fortifications."

Chapter XVI.

THE UTES OF WHITE RIVER.

IN 1878 the gold hunters of Colorado found not gold, but silver. There was a rush of emigrants thither, as in 1849 to California. Leadville grew at the rate of 300 persons a day. Mining camps became thick as leaves and small towns sprang up like magic. Onward rolled the surge of migration till it beat against the barriers of the Ute reservations. Then arose the cry "the Utes must go!" Their lands were suspected of being rich in minerals. They were only Indians, and therefore in the way. Any other reservation would be good enough for them.

In 1879 the Utes were strong in numbers, well armed and rich in horses. The mining population started a furore which had for its object the expulsion of these Indians. Men organized at many points to ward off imaginary attacks. They invented excuses for warlike demonstrations and conjured up grievances to be avenged. The Utes had never been severely hostile. Their country was not affected by any of the great trans-continental thoroughfares. Up until 1863 the Government had never thought of making a treaty with them. Even then it would not have been regarded as necessary but for the fact that a fragment of Utes had been persuaded by the Navajos and Apaches to join them in marauding expeditions. This treaty of 1863 secured to the Utes their native lands in Western Colorado. In 1868 another treaty was made which set apart a larger reservation for the entire Ute family, consisting of seven tribes or bands. There were several agencies on the reservation, but the principal one was on White River. It had ever been the desire of the Utes to have a country of their own and in giving it to them the United States made its dedication most solemn.

Scarcely had the Utes received their first payments under the treaty when the mines in the San Juan Country were discovered and miners flocked in regardless of the fact that they were trespassers on the reservation. A conflict occurred, which was settled by the diplomatic old Chief Ouray, who agreed to cede a mining strip in the San Juan and Miguel Countries, provided the lines of the strip did not cut off any part of the Uncompahgre Park. This cession was ratified by Congress in 1874. Ouray's fears that his method of preserving peace would not be justified by the future were speedily realized. The Indians were outrageously cheated in this deal. The government did not keep its promise to pay $25,000 annually forever for the ceded lands. The lines of the ceded lands were so arranged as to deprive the Utes of some of their best farming lands and as they ran nearly through the centre of the Uncompahgre Park, the Indians received no equivalent lands in any other direction.

Before the Indians could ascertain the magnitude of their loss or take any steps to rectify the boundaries of their cession, their best farming lands around the mining towns were occupied by settlers who refused to move. In 1877 an order was issued by the War Department to remove the intruders by force. Secretary Schurz weakened on the order, and gave the intruders six months time. In the Spring of 1878 a similar order was issued, but by this time the settlers were numerous and defiant. They threatened to precipate an Indian war if they were interfered with then.

A commission was organized to look into the difficulty. It was found that most of the defiant settlers could be appeased if the Government would undertake to quiet their titles to about four square miles of territory. The commission therefore offered to buy from the Utes enough to satisfy the present desires of the settlers, and at the same time settle all troubles about the former cessions. The Utes were stubborn and the commission failed. But a delegation of Utes was brought to Washington the next winter, and, under the influence of the Capitol atmosphere, they were induced to acquiesce in the wishes of the settlers and part with their lands.

These are a few of the events which helped to sour the Utes against the whites. Within the reservation were factions. Some clung to Chief Ouray, others repudiated his authority. The White River Utes hardly recognized him. The agent there, for reasons best known to himself, changed the agency to a point fifteen miles down the river. The White River's flew into a rage about it, and the agent, not understanding their character, attempted to sustain himself by playing off one Indian faction against another. This incensed the Indians all the more. Their umbrage became centered on the agent, whom they accused of wishing to interfere with their customs and privileges and of a design to turn a nation of hunters into ordinary plowmen.

One of their number asssaulted the agent and would have killed him but for the interference of his employees. The agent wrote to Governor

Pitkin for help, and gave it out that nothing but force would prove equal to an occasion in which all the Indians sympathized. In response to the agent's request, three companies of cavalry and one of infantry marched from Fort Fred. Steele toward the Ute reservation. They were commanded by Major Thornburg, and while at the Bear River Crossing, they were met by Chiefs Jack, Colorow and three other Utes. They asked why he was coming. When told that he had been sent for by the agent, they denied all his reports, denied the right of the troops to enter the reservation and asked that the Major go, with five companions, and ascertain for himself how matters stood. The Major said he was under orders, and could only obey them. The Indians then went to the agent and asked him to stop the troops. He said it was none of his business, but on second thought he requested the Major to encamp outside of the reservation and come on with an escort. But unfortunately the troops had already entered the reservation at Red Canyon and were beginning to pass down the canyon. The Indians were in ambush along the bushy edges of the ravine. When they were discovered a parley was sought, in order that hostilities might be averted. Chief Jack had started from the Ute camp, with a similar object in view. The parleying parties never met, for firing began as soon as the troops made their appearance on the upland.

The Indians proved to be in strong force. Captain Payne threw his company into skirmish line on the left, and Captain Lawson on the right. The wagon train was ordered to pack. The Indians pressed the troops hotly. They massed to cut off the retreat of the whites and Major Thornburg ordered his troops to fall back on the wagon train. In executing this movement the Major was killed. Captain Payne took command and instantly set the troops to fortifying. Pick and shovel went to work. Dead horses were piled up as breast-works. Sacks of feed and bedding became bulwarks for sharp shooters. The men worked and fought nobly amid the groans of the wounded and dying. The crack of the Indian rifle was heard on every hand. The sage brush and grass took fire and the flames crept up toward the breastworks of the troops. There was no water and the troopers were forced to drop their tools and weapons and smother the fire with their blankets. Some of their wagons took fire and were saved with difficulty. The situation was a desperate one, but when the smoke lifted the very element that had proved so alarming turned out to be a source of protection. The burning of the sedge had destroyed the cover of the Indians and they were forced to seek the shelter of the bluffs which were some 400 yards distant. While they still commanded the situation they could do but little harm with their rifles at that range.

Word of the battle was sent to the agency Indians who kept it a secret from the agent, in whom they had lost all confidence. They believed the agent had deceived them as to Major Thornburg's expedition and intentions, and so resolved to meet treachery with treachery. That night they held a war dance. The agent sent a message next morning to Major Thornburg, not knowing he had been killed, and the carrier was escorted by two Indians. A few miles out the carrier was killed by his escort, Antelope and Ebenezer, who hastened back to the agency. Meanwhile the Indians there had broken into the storeroom and helped themselves to agency guns and ammunition. Twenty of them then started out to meet Antelope and Ebenezer. When they had met them all returned and immediately opened fire on the agency. Several of the employees fell at the first fire, and the rest with their families sought the cover of the respective houses. The battle raged at intervals throughout the day, the Indians plundering the stores during the lulls. At night they fired several of the buildings. This drove men, women and children from their covers, and in the indiscriminate firing which followed many of the women and children were shot. The rest, including the agents wife, were taken captive. The wreck of the agency was complete.

Chief Ouray was out on a hunting expedition with his band while these atrocities were going on. On hearing of them he returned at once to Los Pinos and prepared an order to the White River Chiefs to stop fighting. Its bearer, Joseph Brady, bore it to the hostiles who at once agreed to obey. Brady also communicated with the soldiers, who were still holding desperately to their position near the mouth of the Red Canyon. They had been re-inforced by Dodge's company of colored troops, who were doing good work in strengthening the fortifications. Further re-inforcements came in under Colonel Merritt, who took entire command. He found that the losses thus far footed up 13 killed and 43 wounded. The Indians were preparing to engage Merritt when Ouray's order reached them. There was no more regular fighting, though several valuable lives were lost in desultory skirmishing.

Very soon Merritt marched his command to White River Agency. All along his line of march were evidences of the fury of the Indians, in the shape of dead bodies, and the agency was a scene of desolation. Every building, except one, had been burned. No sign of life appeared and the ground was strewn with articles of every kind. Every here and there were the bodies of the victims. The body of the agent was found one hundred yards from his house with a bullet hole through his brain, a barrel stave thrust into his mouth and a chain around his neck. The burial of the dead, some of whose bodies had been eaten by wolves, occupied the time of the troops for a day after their arrival.

The next object was to recover the captive women. Special agent Adams was sent with an escort of 15 Utes to the camp of the hostiles to effect their release. The hostiles gave them a stormy welcome. Some were in favor of surrendering them and keeping peace, the rest wished to kill Adams and go on with the war. Fortunately the wife of one of the hostiles was a sister of Ouray, and the wife of another had been cured of a serious illness by Mrs. Meeker, wife of the agent at White River. These stood out for the release of the captives. All in all, peaceful counsels got the upper hand, and the captives were released. They stated that they had been treated with consideration by their captors.

There was now no futher use for the troops on the reservation and they were withdrawn. Subsequently two commissions appointed to investigate the trouble and demand the surrender of the ring-leaders for punishment, sat through tedious sessions. They could get no satisfaction and arrived at no conclusion. But the upshot of the whole affair was that in 1880, the Utes were given seperate reservations, according to their bands, and those of the White River were placed under the jurisdiction of the Uintah Agency.

Chapter XVII.

MESSIAH CRAZE AND GHOST DANCE.

EVEN with Indians, a war must have a reason. We may call the recent demonstrations by the Sioux and kindred tribes, a craze, an uprising, a war, or by what name we please; it is fuller of meaning for the white race and for the Federal Government than anything that goes to make the weird chapters of Indian annals. And it is being studied, too, from many standpoints, all of which are sources of light.

For many months we read of Indian disturbances in the neighborhood of the Pine Ridge reservation, a reservation devoted to the powerful Sioux tribe, or such of it as can be induced to stay on it. These disturbances grew more frequent and pronounced. They extended more widely, till they embraced several of the neighboring tribes who are akin to the Sioux. By and by the various reservations seemed to be ablaze with excitement. The Indians left their reservations and began to cluster as armed bands. There was every evidence of a great conspiracy for some bloody purpose. Settlers left their homes and rushed to the agencies and forts for protection. States and the general Government put their troops on a war footing. It looked as though there might be a gigantic and bloody Indian war. But preparation proved to be timely, thanks to large facilities for transportation and a wise concentration of forces.

The Sioux represent one of the largest and bravest tribes of the Northwest. For thirteen years, what may be called the respectable portion of the tribe, has lived on its reservation, has come to own horses and cattle, and has sent many of its children to eastern schools for an education. It is a tribe in which missionaries have worked with success, and have imparted a fair degree of moral culture and Christian doctrine. Therefore, it is hardly to be expected that it would plunge into war without a reason.

The real beginning of the uprising dates from the visit of the Sioux to the Utes in Utah. The religion of the Utes is a graft of Christianity on their own mythology, and one of its solemnities is the superstitious dance, resembling the Sun dance of old.

But although this dance was brought back with the Sioux, it was, when in its infancy, purely of a religious character, and it was only when the medicine men and politicians in the nation began to enlarge upon the wrongs suffered at the hands of the whites, the scarcity of food, the presence of the military, that its general aspect was changed from the sacred rite to a warlike demonstration. But for these complications and the lack of prompt action on the part of prominent officials, the craze might have been easily suppressed, and the dancers returned to their camps on the agency creeks without any trouble whatever.

The Indians located in the Dakotas have been in the habit of visiting the Utes and Arrapahoes every summer for the purpose of trading and hunting *en route*. While the Sioux are unable to converse with these tribes, means of communication is possible through the medium of the sign-language, which is well understood by all Indians throughout the West. Keeps the Battle (Kicizapi Tawa) relates that it was during the visit of the Pine Ridge Sioux, in July, 1890, that he first heard of the coming of the new Messiah. His story as told by a correspondent of the "*Illustrated American*," which periodical we must also credit with other valuable facts in connection with the Messiah craze, is as follows:—

"Scarcely had my people reached the Ute village when we heard of a white preacher whom the Utes held in the highest esteem, who told a beautiful dream or vision of the coming of a great and good red man. This strange person was to set aright the wrongs of my people; he could restore to us our game and hunting-grounds, was so powerful that every wish or word he gave utterance to became fulfilled.

His teachings had a strange effect upon the Utes, and, in obedience to the commands of this man, they began a Messiah Dance. My people did not pay much attention to this dance at first, and it was not until we took our departure that the matter began to weigh heavily upon the minds of a number in the party. As we left the Ute camp the minister stood with uplifted hands and invoked the blessing of the Great Spirit upon us. He told us to look for the coming of the Saviour, and assured us that he would soon and unexpectedly arrive. He further cautioned us to be watching and ready to accompany him to the bright and Happy Hunting Grounds, to be sorry for our sins, to institute a Messiah Dance among our people at Pine Ridge, and to keep up this dance until the Lord himself should appear."

Immediately upon the arrival of the hunting-party at Pine Ridge, a small dance was held in imitation of the ones they had seen while among the Utes, but until the medicine men began to superintend the ceremonies nothing unusual occurred. The dances were held every few days

GEN. NELSON A. MILES.

until the middle of August. Then, with scarcely any warning, a wild and general desire took possession of a large part of the nation to welcome the expected Messiah the moment he set foot upon earth. The agent, then at the agency, fearing that the enthusiasm of the Sioux might terminate in an outbreak, visited White Bird's camp accompanied by fourteen Indian police. As he approached the village, twenty savage fellows sprang out of the brush, and, drawing their Winchesters, called upon him to halt. They would not permit him to advance, and compelled the party to turn about and retrace its footsteps to the agency, threatening death should Galagher attempt to interfere with their dance.

The news of this bold action spread like wildfire through the country, and, being heralded and exaggerated by the daily press, caused many an uneasy and timid settler to prepare his goods for shipment to the nearest point upon the railroad.

The news of the failure of the agent to stop the Messiah Dance was carried by couriers to the Indians at Rosebud and Standing Rock Reservations, and the more susceptible Indians became infatuated with the new fad. Meetings and dances were arranged at points distant from the agency posts, in order that no employee might interfere. Of course, both the Sioux and the whites were much excited. The former were ready and willing to throw off forever the odious yoke of oppression; the latter, fearful for the safety of their homes and families. If the dances continued to be religious and there was nothing of a warlike nature introduced, there could be no objection to the Sioux dancing as long and as hard as they desired. But older residents, and those acquainted with Indian warfare, knew well that an outbreak was always preceded by a series of dances. While these men were quite familiar with Indian nature, they failed to discern between a religious ceremony and a war dance. Hence the very grave error followed of accusing many friendly Indians, who had joined the dance for no other purpose than worship, of hostile intentions. This accusation, coupled with the arrival of some four or five times as many troops as were necessary to subdue the small number of lodges which later fled into the borders of the Bad Lands, had the effect of turning the more timid toward the agency, while the braver middle-aged and young men fled to the northward.

The aged Red Cloud, a chief of the Sioux, thus describes the beginning of the Messiah craze:—

"We felt that we were mocked in our misery. We had no newspapers and no one to speak for us. We had no redress. Our rations were again reduced. You who eat three times each day, and see your children well and happy around you, can't understand what starving Indians feel. We were faint with hunger and maddened by despair. We held our dying children, and felt their little bodies tremble as their souls went out and left only a dead weight in our hands. They were not very heavy, but we ourselves were very faint, and the dead weighed us down. There was no hope on earth, and God seemed to have forgotten us. Some one had again been talking of the Son of God, and said He had come. The people did not know; they did not care. They snatched at the hope. They screamed like crazy men to Him for mercy. They caught at the promises they heard He had made."

It is quite natural to suppose that the agent was not a little frightened at his reception near "White Bird's" camp, and, as subsequent events would seem to indicate, he feared to assert his authority and compel the Sioux to discontinue their dance. He hoped that in time the craze would die out without interference on his part. But, instead of ceasing, the numbers participating increased, and really things began to assume a very threatening aspect.

The dancers were not slow to take advantage of non-interference, and a report gained wide circulation to the effect that their agent was afraid to command the police to arrest the principals in the dance. The medicine men and Indians of the same stamp as the late Sitting Bull addressed the young men somewhat after the following manner:—

"Do you not see that the whites on the reservation are afraid of you? Why do you pray to great Wakantanka to send the Saviour on earth and bring about a change when the remedy lies in your own hands? Be men, not children. You have a perfect right to dance upon your own reservation as much as you please, and you should exercise this right, even if you find it necessary to use your guns. Be brave, and the great and good Wakantanka will aid your arms. Be cowards, and he will be ashamed of you."

When the Ghost or Messiah Dance was first given on Pine Ridge Reservation by the Sioux who had been in Utah on a visit to the Ute Indians, there were many on-lookers. These became interested as the dance proceeded, for such was its influence upon a beholder that he felt an irresistible desire to join the circle.

GHOST DANCE.

The largest camp of the dancers prior to the departure for the north was located on Wounded Knee Creek. Other camps of considerable extent existed upon White Clay Creek, four miles from the agency headquarters, upon Porcupine and Medicine Root streams.

When the medicine men took the Ghost Dance under their charge one man was appointed "High Priest," to have entire control of the ceremonies. His four assistants were likewise invested with power to start or stop the dance at will. They were given authority to punish any person who should refuse to obey their commands.

While the priests are employed in their prayers the squaws make a good-sized sweat-house. Poles are stuck in the ground and the tops bent together and securely tied. These saplings are strong enough to bear the weight of several hundred pounds. Over the framework are heaped blankets and robes to such a thickness that no smoke or steam can pass from the interior. A fire is started in a hole in the ground several feet from the small entrance to the sweat-lodge, and twenty or thirty good-sized stones are placed therein to be heated. When these rocks have become sufficiently hot, the young men who are to partake of the bath, strip, with the exception of the breech-clout, and crawl through the door. They seat themselves in a circle, with their feet toward the centre and their backs against the sides of the lodge. The attendant shoves some of the hot stones inside, and the young men pour water from a hide-bucket upon the little stone heap. Steam and vapor arise, completely filling the enclosure. The attendant has meanwhile covered the opening so that no air from the outside may penetrate. As the vapor condenses, the attendant thrusts more stones within, and thus the operation is continued as long as the youths can stand the confinement. The pipe is also smoked during the sweat. When the young men issue from their bath the perspiration is fairly streaming from every pore. If it is not cold weather they plunge into a pool in the creek near by, but if it be chilly they wrap blankets about their bodies. None of the whites and half-breeds who have witnessed these things ever saw a Sioux rub himself after issuing from the bath.

Several sweat-houses are erected in order to prepare the young men for the dance. When a good number of young men, say fifty or sixty, have thus prepared themselves, the high-priest and his assistants come forward. The high-priest wears eagle-feathers in his hair, and a short skirt reaches from his waist nearly to his knees.

The assistants are dressed in a similar manner, but wear no ornaments other than the eagle-feathers. The dancers wear no ornaments whatever and enter the circle without their blankets, many of them only wearing their ordinary clothes.

That Indians should lay aside all ornaments and finery, and dance without the trappings which they so dearly love, proves conclusively that some powerful religious influence is at work. In their other dances, the Omaha, the Old Woman, the Sun, and War Dances, feathers and bangles, weapons, herbs or painted and plaited grasses, porcupine quills, horses' tails and bits of fur-skins, necklaces, bells, silver disks, etc., are worn in great profusion.

The candidates for "conversion" do not fast, as has often been stated. After they have come forth from the sweat-house they are ready to enter the sacred circle. The high-priest runs quickly from the village to the open space of ground, five or six hundred yards distant, and stationing himself near the sacred tree, begins his chant as follows:

Hear, hear you all persons.

Come, hurry up and dance, and when you have finished running in the circle, tell these people what you have seen in the spirit land.

I myself have been in the spirit land and have seen many strange and beautiful things, all of which great Wakantanka rules over and which my eyes tell me are good and true.

As the speaker proceeds, the men and women leave their tepees and crowd to the dance-ground. They form two or three circles, according to the number of persons who wish to participate, and, grasping hands with fingers interlocked ("Indian grip"), the circles begin to move around toward the left. They rub their palms in dust or sand to prevent slipping, for it is considered unlucky for one to break connections.

The sacred tree is a nearly straight sapling thirty or forty feet high, trimmed of branches to a height of several feet. To the topmost twigs is attached a small white flag or canvas strip, supposed to be an emblem of purity, together with some of colors. The base of the tree is wrapped with rushes and flags to a thickness of about five feet. Between the reeds the dancers from time to time thrust little gifts or peace-offerings. These offerings are supposed to allay the anger of the Great Spirit, and are given in perfectly good faith by the poor natives. They consist of small pieces of calico, bags of tobacco or pipes. During the heat of excitement, those worshippers most deeply affected cut small parti-

[From Illustrated American.]
FRONT OF THE COMPANY STREET 1st U. S. CAVALRY AT FORT KEOGH.

cles of flesh from their arms, and thrust these, also, between the rushes of the holy tree.

As the circle moves toward the left, the priest and his assistants cry out loudly for the dancers to stop a moment. As they pause he raises his hands towards the west, and upon all the people acting similarly, begins the following remarkable prayer:

Great Spirit, look at us now. Grandfather and Grandmother have come. All these good people are going to see Wakantanka, but they will be brought safely back to earth. Everything that is good you will see there, and you can have these things by going there. All things that you hear there will be holy and true, and when you return you can tell your friends how spiritual it is.

As he prays, the dancers cry aloud with all the fervor of religious fanatics. They moan and sob, many of them exclaiming: "Great Father, I want you to have pity upon me."

One can scarcely imagine the terrible earnestness of these people. The scene of the dance, especially at night, is most weird and ghost-like. The fires are very large, and shed a bright reflection all around. The breasts of the worshippers heave with emotion; they groan and cry as if they were suffering great agony, and as the priest begs them to ask great Wakantanka to forgive their sins, such a cry of despair and anguish arises as to deeply affect even the whites present.

After prayer and weeping, and offerings have been made to the sacred pole, the dance is started again. The dancers go rather slowly at first, and as the priests in the centre begin to shout and leap about, the dancers partake of the enthusiasm. Instead of moving with a regular step, each person jumps backward and forward, up and down, as hard as he or she can without relinquishing their hold upon their neighbor's hand. One by one the dancers fall out of the ranks, some staggering like drunken men, others wildly rushing here and there almost bereft of reason. Many fall upon the earth to writhe about as if possessed of demons, while blinded women throw their clothes over their heads and run through brush or against trees. The priests are kept busy waving eagle-feathers in the faces of the most violent worshippers. The feather is considered sacred, and its use, together with the mesmeric glance and motion of the priest, soon causes the victim to fall into a trance or deep sleep. Whether this sleep is real or feigned the writer does not pretend to say, but sufficiently deep is it that whites visiting the dance have been unable to rouse the sleepers by jest or blow.

Unquestionably the priests exercise an influence over the more susceptible of the dancers akin to hypnotism. One of the young men, who danced in the ghost circle twenty times, narrates that the priest "Looked very hard at us. Some of the young men and women could not withstand his snake-like gaze, and did whatever he told them."

Regarding what is seen by the converts when in the spirit land there is much speculation.

Little Wound gives his experience thus: "When I fell in the trance a great and grand eagle came and carried me over a great hill, where there was a village such as we used to have before the whites came into the country. The tepees were all of buffalo hides, and we made use of the bow and arrow, there being nothing of white man's manufacture in the beautiful land. Nor were any whites permitted to live there. The broad and fertile lands stretched in every direction, and were most pleasing to my eyes.

I was taken into the presence of the great Messiah, and he spoke to me these words:

"My child, I am glad to see you. Do you want to see your children and relations who are dead?"

I replied: "Yes, I would like to see my relations who have been dead a long time." The

God then called my friends to come up to where I was. They appeared, riding the finest horses I ever saw, dressed in superb and most brilliant garments, and seeming very happy. As they approached, I recognized the playmates of my childhood, and I ran forward to embrace them while the tears of joy ran down my cheeks.

We all went together to another village, where there were very large lodges of buffalo hide, and there held a long talk with the great Wakantanka. Then he had some squaws prepare us a meal of many herbs, meats, and wild fruits and "wasna" (pounded beef and choke-cherries). After we had eaten, the Great Spirit prayed for our people upon the earth, and then we all took a smoke out of a fine pipe ornamented with the most beautiful feathers and porcupine quills. Then we left the city and looked into a great valley where there were thousands of buffalo, deer, and elk feeding.

After seeing the valley, we returned to the city, the Great Spirit speaking meanwhile. He told me that the earth was now *bad* and *worn out;* that we needed a new dwelling-place where the rascally whites could not disturb us. He further instructed me to return to my people, the Sioux, and say to them that if they would be constant in the dance and pay no attention to the whites

TEPEES OF SIOUX CHIEFS AT FORT THUNDER.

(From Illustrated American.)

he would shortly come to their aid. If the high priests would make for the dancers medicine shirts and pray over them, no harm could come to the wearer; that the bullets of any whites that desired to stop the Messiah Dance would fall to the ground without doing any one harm, and the person firing such shots would drop dead. He said that he had prepared a hole in the ground filled with hot water and fire for the reception of all white men and non-believers. With these parting words I was commanded to return to earth."

There are intermissions every hour in the progress of the dance, and during these pauses several pipes are passed around. Each smoker blows a cloud upward toward the supposed dwelling-place of the Messiah. He inhales deep draughts of the fragrant smoke of red willow-bark into his lungs, blows it out through his nose, and then passes the pipe to his neighbor.

The songs are sung without accompaniment or a drum, as is customary in the other dances. All sing in unison, and the notes, although wild and peculiar, being in a minor key, do not lack melody.

Just after the dancers have been crying and moaning about their sins the priests strike up the first song, in which all join, singing with deafening loudness. Some man or woman may be at this moment at the tree, with his or her arms thrown about the rushes, sobbing as if the heart would break; or another may be walking and crying, wringing his hands, or going through some motion to indicate the deepest sorrow for his transgressions. So the singer cries aloud to his mother to be present and aid him. The appeal to the father refers, of course, to the Messiah, and its use in this connection is supposed to give emphasis to the demand for the mother's presence and hasten her coming.

The second song expresses in brief the goodness of the father. Some one of the dancers has come to life from the trance, and has just related his or her experience in the other world. The Messiah, or Father, has been very near to the subject, and the high-priest, enlarging upon the importance of this fact, runs about the interior of the circle handing several pipes around, exclaiming that these pipes were received direct from the Great Spirit, and that all who smoke them will live. The people are worked up to such a pitch of religious frenzy that their minds are now willing to receive any utterance as truth undisputable, so they pass around the pipes, singing the song meanwhile. The repetition of the words, "This the father said," gives more weight to the song.

One of the visions seen by a young woman, when under the influence of the trance, varied somewhat from the others. Her story runs thus:—

"I was carried into the beautiful land as others have been, and there I saw a small but well-made lodge constructed entirely of rushes and reeds. These were woven closely together and resembled the fine basket-work that many of our squaws make during the winter. The tepee was provided with a stone wall, which was composed of small, flat stones laid up against the wall to the height of three or four feet. In this lodge the great Wakantanka dwelt and would issue forth at noon. Promptly at the time when the sun was above me the lodge trembled violently and then began its descent toward the earth. It landed near the dance-ground, and there stepped forth a man clothed in a blanket of rabbit-hides. This was the Messiah, and he had come to save us."

The vision of Little Horse is still more remarkable.

"Two holy eagles transported me to the Happy Hunting Grounds. They showed me the Great Messiah there, and as I looked upon his fair countenance I wept, for there were nail-prints in his hands and feet where the cruel whites had once fastened him to a large cross. There was a small wound in his side also, but as he kept himself covered with a beautiful mantle of feathers this wound only could be seen when he shifted his blanket. He insisted that we continue the dance, and promised me that no whites should enter his city nor partake of the good things he had prepared for the Indians. The earth, he said, was now worn out and it should be re-peopled.

He had a long beard and long hair and was the most handsome man I ever looked upon."

The personal experience of the Weasel may be of interest:

"While dancing I saw no visions, but the other Indians told me to not think of anything in particular, but keep my eyes fastened upon the priests, and soon I would see all that they saw.

"The first large dance held was on Wounded Knee Creek under the guidance of Big Road. I attended this one, but did not observe Two Strike in the audience. We had been dancing irregularly for several weeks when a runner came into camp greatly excited, one night, and said that the soldiers had arrived at Pine Ridge and were sent by the Great Father at Washington. The priests called upon the young men at this juncture not to become angry but to continue the dance, but have horses ready so that all could flee were the military to charge the village. So we mounted our ponies and rode around the hills all night singing our two songs. Never before in the history of the "Dakotas" (the name by which the Sioux call themselves, meaning "allies") has a dance like this been known. We did not carry our guns nor any weapon, but trusted to the Great Spirit to destroy the soldiers."

When there is no night dance the Sioux pass the time playing a new and favorite game called "stick guess." It is very simple, for there is nothing used save a short stick held in the clinched hand. The Indian making a wager that he can signify in which hand the stick is concealed, points to the palm beneath which he thinks the stick lies. If he wins, besides the wager he receives a larger portion of dog soup than the others.

Speaking of the situation at Pine Ridge, at the dawn of the Messiah craze, an able correspondent says; —" Had the agency employees and their head acted in concert, and asserted the authority given them by the Commissioner of Indian Affairs, the whole matter could have been settled without great trouble. Philanthropists, while meaning well, from a lack of knowledge of the nature of an Indian treat him in such a sympathetic manner—often selecting the most worthless and lazy Indians to bestow their favors upon—that he becomes puffed up with his own importance. Egotism leads to insolence, and insolence gets him into serious trouble with the agency employees and Westerners in general. The Catholics, Episcopalians, and Presbyterians are all doing a good work, and it is not my purpose to say much against them; but they should work in unison, not against each other. The Indian cannot understand how so many beliefs could spring from one good book, and, naturally suspicious, when he hears one missionary speak disparagingly of the salvation afforded by a rival church, concludes the whole set are humbugs.

When the commission visited the agency in the summer of 1889, for the purpose of securing signatures to the treaty whereby the Sioux relinquished claim to several million acres of their land, a number of promises were made by the commissioners which were never kept. The gentlemen, returning to Washington, engrossed with the many political cares and social pleasures of the capital city, soon forgot the sacred promises assured to the Sioux. Not so with the Indians themselves. As they sat about their tepee fires and discussed the affairs of their nation, they

[From Illustrated American.]

BEAR-COMES-BACK-AGAIN.

often wondered why the increase in rations did not come, why the presents were so long delayed.

An Indian never forgets a promise.

Can it be wondered, then, that the Sioux lost what little remaining faith they had in the whites?

As they brooded over their wrongs, the scarcity of rations, and the miserable treatment of Red Cloud, the man who has taken a firm stand in favor of the whites, the Messiah craze came. Imagine with what joy they hailed the coming of Him who was to save and rescue them. How they hoped and prayed, only to be deluded and again cast into the depths of despair! Even this last boon and comfort was refused by their conquerors; for no sooner had the news of the coming Saviour reached the ears of the Great Father at Washington than he ordered his soldiers to the frontier to suppress the worship of any Indian, who should dare to pray to his God after the dictates of his own conscience."

All through the summer and fall of 1890 the ghost dances became more frequent and intensified, and the Messiah craze ran like a prairie fire through the various tribes of the North. Tribes of the same tongue and recognized as of one blood, which had been hostile to one another, became friends. A general desertion of their reservations took place, followed, very naturally by a concentration of the tribes, the general direction being towards the seats of the more powerful Sioux, and the effect being to make their agency at Pine Ridge a centre of activities. The movements of these excited bodies were mysterious. The nature of their demonstrations were not understood. Excitement was rife in all the white settlements and a feeling of alarm pervaded all the agencies. Rumors spread in all directions, of the wildest sort. The Indians mingled tales of their hard treatment with their religious songs, and their religious dances assumed more and more the form of war dances. They appeared in them fully armed, dressed in war paint and feathers, covered with their ghost shirts which were believed to be impervious to bullets. The spirit of fatalism spread and they courted death at the hands of white men, believing that it would be a speedy transport to a happier sphere. While they abstained from a formal declaration of war, from organized hostility, murders and depredations became frequent. The running off of live stock from the neighborhood of the agencies and settlements was a sport which had special attractions for the young bucks whose infatuation had gained control. The situation was decidedly volcanic, and no one knew what circumstance might precipitate bloody war in the twinkling of an eye.

There was no course for the Government except to be prepared for the worst, hence began the concentration of troops. This work was hastened just in proportion as the power of the Indian police weakened. The Indians grew more defiant of orders to go back to their reservations. They sullenly withdrew from the neighborhood of the agencies, and betook themselves to the mountainous and inaccessible "bad-lands," where they could deliberate secretly, dance at will, and be secure against attack; or, whence they could issue in formidable strength in case war were determined on. The Dakotas, therefore, became a scene of martial activity, seldom witnessed, and the attention of the whole country was attracted toward the Northwest. It was a winter scene, too, and that made it all the more interesting.

The first snows of winter fell on the tents of one cavalry and two infantry regiments, encamped at Pine Ridge; one cavalry and one infantry regiment at the mouth of the Belle Fouche in S. W. Dakota; one infantry regiment at Fort Pieire and one at Fort Yates, while one cavalry and two infantry regiments were placed in camp at Fort Keogh, the scene of many bloody fights, and the spot where General Miles forced the surrender of the fiery Cheyennes in 1877.

It was fortunate that these forces, and those which were to co-operate with them, were under the command of an officer like General Miles, a born Indian fighter, a thorough student of Indian character, and a man in whom the humanities have a large place. When his policy developed it was seen to take the shape of a firm presentation of force, without seeming to use force. The moral effect of well armed and disciplined numbers would win the most decisive victory, because bloodless, if only those untimely provocations which start an avalanche or explode a powder mill could be avoided for a sufficient length of time.

The position of the troops was in the nature of a cordon, which could be relaxed or tightened, as circumstances required. Thus the whole scene of activity was, under the winter snows, picturesque. The Sibley tents of the white troopers, contrasted in neatness and comfort with the tepees of the Indians, after which they were patterned.

Amid the uncertainties of the hour and the dangers which constantly threatened, camp-life could not grow monotonous, nor could the severest discipline be relaxed for a moment. The American soldier was called upon to do duty in a temperature far below zero. As long as roads could be kept open, the supplies could be had in abundance, through the agency of the government mule teams. It was only when called to go on a distant scout, or in search of a band of renegade Indians, amid one of those peculiar sand blizzards of the region, that the enemy could be certain of any advantage. In all else the Indian was at a decided disadvantage. His tepees were not so warm as the Sibley's. His food supplies were more precarious. His discipline was his infatuation, the coherence of complaint united with frenzy.

The tract of country surrounded by the troops and occupied by the disaffected Indians, was embraced within boundaries made by the Cannon Ball, Missouri and Niobrarra Rivers, and by a line drawn northward through Forts Robinson and Meade to the Cannon Ball. There was no outlet to the East. To the South all was thickly peopled. To the West there was nothing but starvation. To the North was the North Pacific Railroad which could be lined in a few hours with troops for defence. The problem the Indians were gradually made to face was, therefore, extermination if they should grow so infatuated as to attack, or final acquiescence as time gave opportunity for them to cool off. As yet, but little had occurred to resolve the uncertainties of the situation. The camps are flooded with rumors from the respective Indian headquarters, and every demonstration of theirs, no matter what its intent, is heralded as the beginning of atrocities. The whole country is kept in alarm by the wildest stories of expected disaster.

Only by the slowest degrees does General Miles become acquainted with the real situation. He employs his Indian police as scouts and messengers, makes them bearers of information between the camps, uses them to overcome prejudices and to ascertain intentions, and if force become necessary they appear rather as policemen for arrest, than as soldiers for slaughter. And as the General learned of the true inwardness of the situation, he found that notwithstanding the apparent wisdom of his movements and the humanity of his aims, they were, in part, contributing to the discontent of the Indians, for as a casual visitor at Pine Tree might well have asked," why are these two thousand soldiers here, when only four hundred lodges of Sioux and Cheyennes are in sight?" So the Indians asked "why are these soldiers here? We are not for war." The fleeing of the Sioux to the edge of the bad lands was not that they might prepare for war, but that they might worship their Good Spirit, Wakantanka alone and prepare for the coming of their Messiah, unmolested by the whites. Even friendly Indians were known to express the sentiment that, under the circumstances, the presence of so many white troops was an insult, and an encouragement of the suspicion that the true meaning was to rob the Indians of the miserable remnants of land that had been left them. Little Wound, when compelled by hunger to go to the house of a herder for food, thus expressed himself, "My friend I have asked the Great Father for food for I am hungry, and he has given me none. I am too old to join my brothers in the North, so I must remain with the squaws at the agency and live on what you see fit to give me."

When nursing a grievance the Indian is sullen and reticent. When suspicious, he is the most difficult being on earth to interview. Hence he contributed but little directly to an understanding of tribal intentions, though much indirectly as his laments crept more fully into his songs, and his grievances tinged his harrangues. He would almost refuse to charge that the beef ration due the reservation had been diminished a million pounds a year, even though the population on the reserve had increased, yet this startling fact would creep out in his songs and murmurs, and would be talked over around the council fires.

Nor would he openly charge that the beef cattle issued to them in the winter were smaller or thinner than those in summer, but the shameful fact was no less a source of profound discontent. Again, only by persistent inquiring based on actual visits to the lodges, by Indians of friendly disposition, could it be fully ascertained how deep the indignation was in the bosoms of all the tribes against the whites, for the unjust assumption that their fervor as exhibited in the Ghost dance, and their faith as manifested in the Messiah expectation, were not real, but a possible cloak for dissatisfaction and a prelude to war.

It is, of course, easy to deny everything from the Indian's standpoint; just as easy as for society to turn up its nose at the overwrought pictures of Dickens. Yet no one can read Dickens without a good deal more than a half consent. Yellow Hair's story may be discounted by as much as you please of white sentiment, but you cannot obliterate its effect entirely, nor deny it a place among the touching episodes of aboriginal life. He said, "Little Wound's daughter had been sick in the lodge for several days. She had no food, nor had any of her friends. She begged for meat, or broth, or bread. Little Wound could not withstand the heart-rending appeals of his dying daughter. He started for

VIEW OF THE BAD-LANDS.

the agency to beg food from the agent; when a few rods away his squaw came running out of the lodge crying, "toiyanka! toiyanka! come back! come back!" He returned with fear and trembling—his poor child was dead. As she died she said, "Oh, give me food, just a little food!" Falling back on the couch she died, then Little Wound drew himself up to his full stature and said "I would fight if my young men were bold and avenge the death of my child!"

The first reliable information regarding the location of the camps of the hostiles was brought into headquarters about the middle of December, 1890. The heroic messenger was a Louis Shangraux, of French and Indian descent, who had gone forth into the unknown at the head of thirty-two Indian companions, for the purpose of finding out something definite about the location and intentions of the ghost dancing tribes.

Louis' party had been selected for its mission because the regular government scouts had failed to reach the camp site of two of the most important chiefs, Short Bull and Kicking Bear, and because their reports were considered generally unreliable. He had been left to his choice of men, and had chosen thirty-two good and reliable friendly Indians, whom he could depend on in case of trouble. No white men went with them, for it was believed the hostiles would kill any one not an Indian who should venture near the camp. From subsequent events this was found to be true.

The country through which they rode presented a similiar appearance to a volcanic region. Great fissures yawned on all sides, peaks of gray-colored earth, or a dirty whitish, limestone bluff towered here and a precipice extended there. The trees become stunted as one advanced, and the grass disappeared. Finally all vegetation vanished and there remained naught but a series of peaks, of deep valleys, of horrible pits suggestive of the road to the infernal regions! Truly a more fitting place for an Indian massacre could not have been found in the United States. Occasional broader valleys afforded a stunted growth of grass for ponies, but these fertile spots were great distances apart and of limited extent. In prehistoric times eruptions of the submerged volcanoes, or shrinkages in the earth's crust caused the irregularities, which everywhere existed. Louis says "that the country affords splendid places for ambuscades—little amphitheatres, as it were, with but one entrance, the sides of which are so irregular as to form good hiding-places for lurking savages. The hostiles' fort cannot be approached except through about five miles of such land.

While in the hostile camp, Louis became an eye witness of the ghost dance.

The dancing continued for nearly thirty hours; then there was an intermission of several hours, during which a council was held in order to give audience to the peace commission. Short Bull and Two Strike, aided by Crow Dog, took the side of the hostiles, while No Neck and Louis Shangraux spoke in behalf of the friendlies. Louis said that, "the agent would forgive you if you would return now, and would give you more rations but not permit you to dance." To this Short Bull (Tatankaptecelan) replied:—

"I have risen to-day to tell you something of importance. You have heard the words of the brothers from the agency camps, and if you have done as myself you have weighed them carefully. If the Great Father would permit us to continue the dance, would give more rations, and quit taking away portions of the reservation, I would be in favor of returning. But even if you (turning to Louis) say that he will, how can we discern whether you are telling the truth? We have been lied to so many times that we will not believe any words that your agent sends to us. If we return he will take away our guns and ponies, put some of us in jail for stealing cattle and plundering houses. We prefer to stay here and die, if necessary, to loss of liberty. We are free now and have plenty of beef, can dance all the time in obedience to the command of Great Wakantanka. We tell you to return to your agent and say to him that the Dakotas in the Bad Lands are not going to come in."

The gathering broke up, and nearly every one continued in the ghost dance. For two days the hostiles would not have further words with the friendly scouts.

About noon, Saturday, Two Strike—who had been one of the leaders in the dance—arose and announced his intention to return to the agency with the scouts, accompanied by about one hundred and forty-five lodges. Crow Dog (Kangi Sunka, the Indian who killled Spotted Tail about ten years ago) also announced his intention of returning. At this declaration from two such prominent men, Short Bull sprang to his feet and cried out angrily:

"At such a time as this we should all stick together like brothers. Do not leave; remain with us. These men from the agency are not telling us the truth; they will conduct you back to the agency and they will place you in jail there.

Louis is at the bottom of this affair. *I know he is a traitor ; kill him, kill him !*

With clubbed guns many of the desperate youths rushed upon the friendlies and scouts, others cocked their Winchesters, and for a few moments it looked as if poor Louis and No Neck, Two Strike and Crow Dog, would lose their lives. Crow Dog sat upon the ground and drew his blanket over his head.

The wiser heads prevailed, however, and after a great hub-bub, in which several young men were knocked down, order was restored. It was during this trouble that Crow Dog made his famous short speech :

"I am going back to White Clay (the location of the agency) ; you can kill me if you want to, now, and prevent my starting. The agent's words are true, and it is better to return than to stay here. I am not afraid to die."

Imagine the surprise of the friendlies when, upon looking back from the top of a ridge two miles distant, they saw the one hundred and seventeen lodges of hostiles coming after them. They halted to wait for Short Bull to catch up, and then the entire outfit moved toward the agency, all happy in the prospect of peace and forgiveness.

But the hopes of the friendlies were short-lived, for Short Bull became scared after having proceeded four miles farther, and, together with his band, left the rear of the column and returned to the Bad Lands.

[From Illustrated American.]
SITTING BULL. (Late Photograph.)

Chapter XVIII.

MASTERING THE SITUATION.

THE events of moment, in connection with the use of the military for the suppression of this unique Indian uprising of 1890, occurred in the following historic order:

By November 14th, 1890, the disquietude among the Sioux Indians, resulting from Sitting Bull's prophecy that a new Messiah was soon to appear to restore to the Indians the land taken from them by the palefaces and to bring back the buffalo, had assumed such proportions that the Interior Department at that date transferred the control of the Indians of North Dakota, under orders of the President, to the War Department, and General Miles was placed in control. Troops were sent forward rapidly, and it was expected that within a short time there would be 3,000 regulars massed in North Dakota. Sitting Bull would be able to bring 3,000 warriors into action in case of trouble, and it was the intention of the War Department to overawe the Indians before they could have a chance of doing anything, by bringing against them an equal force of United States soldiers.

Several years before, there were similiar indications of trouble with the Sioux, and a like course was followed at that time, with such success that the Indians abandoned their proposed attack on the whites, and it was thought that the same result would follow at this time. An actual outbreak was not anticipated by either the officials of the Interior or the War Department, but the situation was sufficiently critical to warrant prompt and extraordinary measures of precaution. General Miles had had great success in dealing with the Indians and it was believed that he would soon convince them of the error of Sitting Bull's prediction.

On Nov. 17th 1890, General Miles received official advices from Fort Custer, Montana, in the shape of a report from the Post Adjutant, Lieut. F. C. Robertson, upon the religious craze as it affected the Cheyennes. Lieut. Robertson says, "On my arrival at the agency, I put myself in immediate communication with Porcupine, the Apostle of the new religion among the Cheyennes and with Big Beaver, who accompanied him on his visit to the new Christ, at Walker Lake, Nevada, last year. When questioned as to the identity of the 15 or 16 tribes who were at the Walker Lake meeting last year, he said they included Cheyennes, Sioux, Arraphoes, Gros Ventres, Utes, Navajoes, Sheep Eater Bannocks and some other tribes whose names he did not know. He says all of the Utah Indians had been there and had left before his arrival.

He is sure there were no tribes from Indian Territory represented, and thinks the Sioux were the most eastern Indians present. He says that he first heard of this new Christ at Arrapahoe (Shoshone Agency), Wyoming, where he and 12 other Cheyennes went on a visit last fall. An Arrapahoe Indian named Sage, who had been to the Southwestern country in 1889, told them that there was a new Christ arisen for the Indians; told where he could be found and explained his doctrine to them. Porcupine goes on to say that he and the other Cheyennes were much interested, and determined to see this Messiah, but, as all could not go so far, nine of the Cheyennes were sent back.

Porcupine and the Cheyennes went on. When they got to Tongue River they crossed to their caravans, Indians joining them in groups at different points *en route*, so that, when the final meeting took place at Walker Lake to hear the Christ speak, there were several hundred Indians present, including women and children. He especially insists that the teachings of the new Christ were in the interest of peace and good order and industry on the part of the Indians."

Appended to this report is the testimony of the Cheyenne Porcupine, in which he describes his journey among the various Indian tribes, seemingly for pleasure and information, and his arrival at length among a fish-eating tribe, supposed to be dwellers on Pyramid Lake, Nevada. That part of his testimony which bears directly upon the uprising is as follows:

"What I am going to say is the truth. The two men sitting near me were with me, and will bear witness that I speak the truth.

I and my people have been living in ignorance until I went and found out the truth. All the whites and Indians are brothers, I was told there. I never knew this before.

The fish-eaters, near Pyramid Lake, told me that Christ had appeared on earth again. They said Christ knew he was coming; that 11 of his children were also coming from a far land. It appeared that Christ had sent for me to go there, and that was why, unconsciously, I took my journey. It had been foreordained. They told me when I got there that my Great Father was there also, but I did not know who he was. The people assembled, called a council, and the chief's

(From Illustrated Americas.)

OFFICERS OF 20TH AND 25TH INFANTRY AT FORT KEOGH.

sons went to see the Great Father, who sent word to us to remain 14 days in that camp, and that then he would come and see us. At the end of two days, on the third morning, hundreds of people gathered at this place. They cleared a place near the agency in the form of a circus ring, and we all gathered there. Just before sundown I saw a great many people (mostly Indians) coming dressed in white men's clothing; the Christ was with them. They all formed in this ring, and around it they put up sheets all around the circle, as they had no tents. Just after dark some of the Indians told me that Christ (Father) was arrived. I looked around to find him, and finally saw him sitting on one side of the ring. He was dressed in a white coat with stripes. The rest of his dress was a white man's, except that he had on a pair of moccasins. Then he commenced our dance, everybody joining in, the Christ singing while we danced. We danced till late in the night, when he told us we had danced enough. The next morning he told us he was going away that day, but would be back the next morning and talk to us. I heard that Christ had been crucified and I looked to see, and I saw a scar on his wrist and one on his face, and he seemed to be the man. I could not see his feet. He would talk to us all day That evening we all assembled to see him depart. When we were assembled he began to sing, and he commenced to tremble all over violently for a while and then sat down. We danced all that night, the Christ lying down beside us, apparently dead.

The following morning the Christ was back with us and wanted to talk to us. He said: 'I am the man who made everything you see around you. I am not lying to you my children. I made this earth and everything on it. I have been to Heaven and seen your dead friends and have seen my own father and mother.' He spoke to us about fighting, and said that it was bad; that we must keep from it; the earth was to be all good hereafter; that we must be friends with one another. He said if any man disobeyed what he ordered, his tribe would be wiped from the face of the earth.

Ever since the Christ I speak of talked to me I have thought what he said was good. I have seen nothing bad in it. When I got back I knew my people were bad and had heard nothing of all this, so I got them together and told them of it, and warned them to listen to it for their own good. I told them just what I have told you here to-day "

By November, 1890, reports began to come from various parts of Dakota, which indicated a scare among the white settlers in various places.

Those from Mandan were of the most excitable nature. Squads of Indians were making raids, burning buildings and looting cattle, the settlers were fleeing in terror and seeking safety at the nearest towns and ports. General Ruger took but little stock in these reports, he regarded them as gross exaggerations, and did not hesitate to say so publicly. " Some of these reports " said he, "are particularly exaggerated, especially those relating to an attack on Mandan.

The Indians located nearest to Mandan are about 35 miles away, on the Cannon Ball River. They are thrifty, industrious, peaceable people, who have taken up claims, built huts and houses, own cattle, ponies and wagons, and are in good circumstances.

They are Christianized Indians, having no faith in aboriginal superstitions and disliking this new Messiah craze, for they say it interferes with the progress of the people. And every year these Indians sell hundreds of thousands of pounds of beef to the Standing Rock Agency, receiving not only a good price therefor, but also some of the beef in return as rations.

Now, you can't convince me that the people who have land, homes, stock, cattle, wagons, crops and revenue are at all anxious to go to war, and yet these are the ones to watch whom the people at Mandan have sent scouts. During my inquiries I found that there was nothing having the appearance of war or indicative of war in this Messianic belief. The Indians say that the whites are to be destroyed, but by Christ alone and without aid from the red man. A mud wave is to engulf the pale faces, but the Indians are to be lifted above it until it passes over. This ghost dance, too, is a harmless affair, being equivalent to Christian communion—that is, a preparatory ceremony through which the participants aim to perfect themselves before the coming of the Master."

Notwithstanding the contradictory character of the rumors that were flying thick and fast, General Miles was busy shifting the troops at his disposal, so as to bring them into the most available positions. The troops at Fort Russell, Wyoming, were placed under orders to move at a moment's notice. The troops at Forts Omaha, Robinson and Niobrarra, were ordered to hold the Indians in check at Pine Ridge and Rosebud agencies, on the Dakota frontier. These orders placed 2,000 troops, well in hand, in less than a week.

On November 19, 1890, General Miles reported the situation, thus: "In my opinion the forces now at hand, and those on the Rosebud and

A HOSTILE ENCAMPMENT.

Pine Ridge agencies will be sufficient to protect the lives and public property at these agencies, and control the Indians there, if they do not commit any serious overt acts before the arrival of the troops, or immediately upon the arrival of this force. I am of the opinion that the presence of the troops will have a most quieting effect. I have received information that night before last 'American Horse,' who is one of the Sioux tribe, had a narrow escape from assassination from the turbulent Indians at the Pine Ridge agency. This Indian is a prominent Sioux chief, and a friend to the United States Government. He has been so regarded for years, and always inclined to be peaceable and loyal.

To nothing but the turbulent, hostile and disaffected spirit of the Indians can I attribute this attempt to murder American Horse. They are seemingly angry because American Horse opposes the turbulent spirit manifested by the Indians and strenuously opposes such actions."

A youth of the Arickaree tribe, who had been educated in one of the Eastern schools, but who was fast relapsing into the ways of his fathers, said that, "the Sioux are in good shape for a fight. They have plenty of guns and ammunition, and also have all the jerked beef they want. The Arickarees are friendly with the whites, and we don't want to fight ourselves, but we would like to see the Sioux go on the war path; because it would mean larger rations for all the Indians in the Dakotas. I don't know whether the Sioux set the recent fires that destroyed so much property, but I believe they did. The Sioux say they have the white man's meat to eat while fighting white men. The Sioux expect the Messiah every day. There are 300 young bucks missing from the reservation. Scouts and Indian police don't know where they are. We are friends of the whites and not of the Sioux, but the Sioux gave us forty ponies, so we will be their friends whatever happens."

On November 20, reports from all sources were wilder than ever. The town of Valentine, Nebraska, was said to be full of fugitives from the country north of the railroad and about the Pine Ridge Agency. The country was thoroughly aroused and all who could get away were fleeing to places of safety. News that the troops had been put on the march was exciting the Indians, and hundreds of braves were withdrawing from the agencies and disappearing in the Bad Lands, which procedure was regarded as ominous.

Advices from Pine Ridge under date of November 21, were to this effect:

The dancing Indians have the agency and the surrounding country in a state of terror. The Ghost dances, under the lead of Little Wound, Six Feathers and other chiefs, are still going on at Wounded Knee creek, White Clay and Medicine, and the Indians have their guns strapped to their backs as they dance. Yesterday a large band of Indians left Rosebud Agency and headed this way. It is within the bounds of possibility that the dancing Indians may consolidate their forces at Wounded Knee, and in that case a fight may be expected at any moment. Medicine Root, the furthest point from the agency where the dancing is going on, is 30 miles away, Wounded Knee is 15 and Porcupine 25.

The wives and children of all the traders and other whites about the agency have left for the safer points along the railroad, and the men here are prepared for the worst.

The last news from Wounded Knee, was to the effect that the Ghost dances were being held nightly and that all the Indians collected there were excited, threatening and boisterous. The rumor that the troops were coming was repeated there and only elicited threats in response. The Indians declared their Messiah was advising them and encouraging them every day and that the dances could not be stopped.

"If the soldiers come here," they said, "we will treat them the way we did the agent and his policemen."

General Miles reported officially as follows: Reliable information has been received that the Yanktons and Grosventres, on the Upper Missouri, also those near old Fort Belknap, have unanimously adopted the Messiah craze; the latter quite ugly; that Sitting Bull has sent emissaries to these tribes and to the 48 lodges of Sioux north of the British line, exciting them to get arms and ammunition and join the other warriors near Black Hills in the spring. Every effort is being made to allay and restrain the turbulent, but the violent overt act of any small party of the desperate ones may cause a general uprising. The latest reports from the Northern Cheyennes is that they have abandoned the delusion. There should be no delay, however, in putting other troops than those in these two departments in proper equipment for the field. Short Bull had risen to the position of prophet or Messiah among the Indians near the Rosebud agency. He grew eloquent at Camp Leaf and thus unburdened himself:

"My friends and relatives: I will soon start the thing in running order. I have told you that this would come to pass in two seasons, but since the whites are interfering so much I will advance

(From Illustrated American.)

INTERIOR OF CAVALRY TENT AT PINE RIDGE.

the time from what my Father above told me. The time will be shorter, therefore you must not be afraid of anything. Some of my relatives have no ears so I will have them blown away. Now there will be a true tree sprout up, and then all the members of your religion and the tribe must gather together. That will be the place where we will see our relatives. But before this time we will have the balance of the moon, at the end of which time the earth will shiver very hard. Whenever this thing occurs I will start the wind to blow. We are the ones who will then see our fathers, mothers and everybody. We are the tribe of Indians and the ones who are living the sacred life. God, our Father, Himself has told and commanded and shown me to do these things. Our Father in heaven has placed a mark at each point of the four winds. First, a clay pipe, which lies at the setting of the sun and represents the Sioux tribe; second, there is a holy arrow lying at the north, which represents the Cheyenne tribe; third, at the rising of the sun there lies hail, representing the Arrapahoe tribe; and fourth, there lies a pipe and nice feather at the south, which represents the Crow tribe. My Father has shown me these things, therefore we must continue the dance. There may be soldiers to surround you, but pay no attention to them.

Continue the dance. If the soldiers surround you four deep, those upon whom I put holy spirits will sing a song which I have taught you, and some of them will drop dead. Then the rest will start to run, but their horses will sink into the earth. The riders will jump from their horses, but they will sink into the earth and you can do what you desire for them.

Now, you must know this—that all the soldiers and the race will be dead. There will be only 500 of them left living on the earth. My friends and relatives, this is straight and true. Now, we must gather at Pass Creek when the tree is sprouting. Then we will go among our dead relatives. You must not take any earthly things with you. Their women and men must disrobe themselves.

My Father above has told us to do this and we must do as he says. You must not be afraid of anything. The guns are the only things that we are afraid of, but they belong to our Father in Heaven. He will see that they do not harm. Whatever white men may tell you do not listen to them; my relations, this is all. I will now raise my hand up to my Father and close what He has said to you through me."

The dispatches of November 24, were to the following effect: Apparently General Miles believes that if the Indians do go on the war path the campaign against them will be a protracted one, for he is moving field artillery, large quantities of ammunition and supplies, as well as cavalry and infantry. Notwithstanding sensational telegrams the army will not take the offensive, but is under orders not to attack the braves until they do something more warlike than dancing. Instructions are to prevent trouble, if possible, by persuading the Indians to return to the agency.

The Messiah craze continued to spread, and by this time it had reached the Cheyennes and Arraphoes as far south as the Indian Territory. A friendly, sent to investigate the situation among the Southern tribes reported that:

"A Sioux Indian, acting as a missionary, has come from the North to teach the new religion to the Southern tribes. He preaches to them that any one who does not believe in the new religion will be destroyed, and in this manner he so works upon the imagination of these people that they fall prostrate to the ground, and while lying there the missionary pretends to cast some spell on them, and when they rise they declare they have seen the new Christ and at once join in the ghost dance, which they keep up until exhausted. This new religion has also spread to the Kiowas, Comanches and Apaches, whose reservation adjoins the Cheyennes and Arrapahoes on the south, and different tribes all join in holding the ghost dance, and are rapidly becoming more restless and desperate as the time for the coming of the new Messiah, who is to lead them to victory, draws near."

The dispatches of November 26, report that the Sioux lodges in the neighborhood of Pine Ridge indicated the presence of about 6,000 Indians, but the bucks were mostly away. The weather was the mildest known for years and was favorable for military operations. The Government had taken into its employ about 1,200 Indian scouts. These were friendlies and were proving to be a very effective force for police purposes. The celebrated Buffalo Bill was given a commission as Brigadier-General and ordered on a scout into the Northwest. Short Bull's camp on White River, at the mouth of Pass Creek, had assumed immense proportions, and its occupants were supposed to number 1,500 warriors, all well armed. They were a surly set, and Gen. Miles saw more difficulty in an attempt to bring him in, than in any other which then confronted him. Little Wound came freely into the agency, and this was regarded as a sure sign that the strength of the disaffected Indians would gradually diminish.

During the month of November the excitement among the white settlers in the vicinity of the uprising continued, and tales of burning, plunder and murder, came into the respective headquarters with great frequency. Many of them proved to be sheer inventions, while others were provoked by indiscreet conduct on the part of those who had been taught to kill an Indian and parley with him afterwards. Nevertheless, there were many real outrages, perpetrated by foolhardy bucks, who had detached themselves from the main force for a purpose of gratifying a propensity for deviltry.

General Miles was fast operating his Indian police force. They were sent out to various Indian camps where the ghost dance was progressing, with orders to arrest the ringleaders and deposit them in jail at the agencies. He also continued to dispose of his forces so as to draw his chain closer around the centres of disturbance.

The dispatches of November, 30, showed a concentration of the hostiles in the vicinity of Wounded Knee. They were supposed to number 1,300 ghost dancing warriors, frenzied with excitement and ready for any deed. The military were held under orders to move at a moment's notice, and it was well understood that Wounded

Knee was to be their destination, where one of the bloodiest fights in Indian history was anticipated. The alarm was increased by the report of Plenty Bear—an old friendly—who had come in from Wounded Knee. His estimate of the hostiles was 2,000 warriors, all in a state of excitement at the efforts of the troops to stop their ghost dances. He said they had taken an oath of resistance if it cost the last drop of their heart's blood. He witnessed one of their dances and saw Little Wound and his band engaged in it, though that chief had promised to stop further indulgence in such demonstrations.

By December 1st, the Government began to change its Indian agents, some of those in position having proved incompetent. Both General Miles and Buffalo Bill had arrived at the conclusion that as Sitting Bull was a leading and perverse spirit, his arrest would tend to bring the agitation to an end. The situation was not nearly so encouraging at this date, and even General Miles despaired of securing terms of the hostiles without a battle. More troops were called for, and the effort to concentrate them so as to be provided for the worst was greater than ever. The language of General Miles at this date is as follows:

"The dissatisfaction is more widespread than it has been at any time for years. The conspiracy extends to more different tribes that have heretofore been hostile but that are now in full sympathy with each other, and are scattered over a larger area of country than in the whole history of Indian warfare.

It is a more comprehensive plot than anything ever inspired by the Prophet Tecumseh, or even Pontaic.

The causes of this difficulty are easy of location. Insufficient food supplies, religious delusions and the innate disposition of the savage to go to war must be held responsible.

All that is possible is being done to encourage the loyal and reduce the number and influence of the hostile, and in this way an outbreak may be averted. I sincerely hope there will be no hostilities, for a general uprising would be a most serious affair.

Altogether there are in the Northwest about 30,000 who are affected by the Messiah craze; that means fully 6,000 fighting men. Of this number, at least one-third would not go on the warpath, so that leaves us with about 4,000 adversaries. There are 6,000 other Indians in the Indian Territory who will need to be watched if active operations take place. Four thousand Indians can make an immense amount of trouble. But a tithe of that number were concerned in the

Minnesota massacre, yet they killed 500 settlers in a very brief space of time.

Altogether, we have about 2,000 mounted men. We have plenty of infantry, but you cannot catch mounted Indians with foot soldiers. The infantry had one or two good fights in 1876 and 1877, but such engagements are rare in frontier warfare.

The Indians are better armed now than they ever were and their supply of horses is all that could be desired. Every buck has a Winchester rifle, and he knows how to use it. In the matter of subsistence they are taking but little risk. They can live on cattle just as well as they used to on buffalo, and the numerous horse ranches will furnish them with fresh stock, when cold and starvation ruin their mounts. The Northern Indian is hardy and can suffer a great deal. These hostiles have been starved into fighting, and they will prefer to die fighting rather than starve peaceably.

I hope the problem may be solved without bloodshed, but such a happy ending to the trouble seems impossible. An outbreak would cost the lives of a great many brave men, and the destruction of hundreds of homes in the Northwest. If peace is possible we will have it."

By this time it had become apparent to Gen. Miles that scarcity of food was not an idle complaint on the part of the Indians. He says:

"We have overwhelming evidence from officers, inspectors and testimony of agents as well, and also from the Indians themselves, that they have been suffering for the want of food, more or less, for two years past, and one of the principal causes of disaffection is this very matter. One of the principal objects of my recent visit to Washington was to urge the necessity of immediate relief, and I am happy to say that success has crowned my efforts.

The Secretary of the Interior has ordered an increase of rations and has asked Congress to appropriate the necessary money. Gen. Brooke telegraphs this morning from Pine Ridge, saying: 'There has been an issue of rations, excepting beef. The orders to the agent at this Agency, from the Secretary of the Interior, increase the Indians' rations but slightly in meat.'"

Word from the Bad Lands, whither most of the hostiles had secluded themselves, ran as follows:

The hostile Indians are making use of every moment's delay on the part of the military to move on them by strengthening their now almost impregnable camp in the dreaded Bad Lands. The 500 or 600 squaws with them are working day and night digging rifle pits about the camp.

This is something very unusual, if not wholly unprecedented, on the part of Indians preparing for war. The reason for this move is, our scouts say, more to insure the protection of the immense quantities of stolen beef and provisions in the camp than to insure a greater slaughter of soldiers. The moment that these supplies are captured by the military that moment the Indians must surrender, unless their thirst for blood is so intense as to lead them to fight until they are downed, either by starvation or United States bullets. At best, whether the military can capture the bulk of the hostiles' supplies or not, the Indians have undoubtedly secreted small quantities sufficient in the aggregate to run them for at least eight or ten weeks.

On December 4, President Harrison received the following memorial from Rosebud agency:

Great Father: This day I will write you a letter with a good heart. When we gave up the Black Hills you told us in that treaty that a man would get three pounds of beef a day. The meaning was three pounds for one man. Besides, you said we could get food just like the soldiers. You did not, however, give it to us at this rate.

Great Father, we are starving, and beg you, therefore, to give to us just so, as you have promised. Thirty men of us; yet us, get for 18 days (only one cow) to eat; that is the reason I mention it. And if you do not well understand you send me (Hollow Horn Bear) traveling money and I will come with five men.

"Great Father, if you do not (want to) do so, then please let us have a soldier for our father (Agent) when our present father's term is out. Great Father, please do us this favor.

Signed by 102 Sioux Indians.

The news from Pine Ridge for December 5, showed no change in the situation. It ran briefly: The hostile Rosebud Indians sleep upon their arms, prepared constantly for an attack. They have three lines of signal couriers between this agency and their camp, and any movement of the troops would be known in a few moments.

They have taken all they wish of the Government's beef herd and burned the buildings and corrals. They are living high and are happy. They have moved to the edge of the Bad Lands. Military preparations proceed rapidly. Unless the Indians come in within a very few days troops will be equipped and in position, when an advance may be ordered.

A scare at Frisco amounted to a panic. Four thousand Indians were encamped on the South Canadian. Settlers from the surrounding country came flocking into the village by scores, and reports of depredations were rife. At Cannon Ball station, Captain Ketchem had an interview with all the Chiefs of the Yanktonnais who could be summoned at short notice, such as Two Bears, Wolf, Necklace, Big Head, Black Tomahawk and Red Fish.

They stated that they had no grievances, and with one accord said the later treaties had been complied with. They expressed grave fears lest the conduct of Bull and others would result in war, and that the Crook-Foster-Warner treaty would be abrogated thereby. They were assured that friendly Indians would not suffer and were content.

On December 7, General Miles thus pictured the situation:—" Generals Ruger and Brooke have been doing all they could to put the small number of available troops in position to be useful, and so far as possible staying the threatened cyclone, yet the end of the Indian troubles is by no means immediately at hand. No other civilized country on earth would tolerate many thousands of armed savages scattered through different States and Territories.

The people of Texas, Western Kansas, Nebraska, North and South Dakota, Montana, Wyoming, Utah, Eastern Washington, Idaho, Arizona and New Mexico are seriously interested in this subject. While the fire may be suppressed in one place, it will be still smouldering and liable to break out at other places where the least expected under the present system."

After great difficulty, Lieutenant Gaston of the 8th Cavalry succeeded in getting a conference with the Cheyennes at the Tongue River Mission. He reported as present, the chiefs Spotted Wolf, Old Crow, White Elk, Bad Gun, Porcupine and a number of other Cheyennes, Sioux, and Fire Crow, an Ogallalah Sioux. The result of the conference was not satisfactory, but it was thought that an appeal to force could be avoided. General Brooke also succeeded in securing an audience with the hostiles who had got beyond reach into the Bad Lands. The chiefs came to the conference bearing a flag of truce and armed with Winchester and Springfield rifles. The entrance of the novel procession produced a flutter of excitement, the greatest that has been known here at the agency since the trouble began.

First came the chiefs, who were Turning Bear, Big Turkey, High Pine, Big Bad Horse and Bull Dog, who was one of the leaders in the Custer massacre. Next came Two Strike, the head chief, seated in a buggy with Father Jute. Surrounding these was a body guard of four young warriors. All the Indians were decorated with war paint and feathers, while many wore ghost dance leggins and the ghost dance shirts dangling at their saddles.

Bunches of eagle feathers were tied on the manes and tails of most of the ponies, while the backs of the docile little animals were streaked with paint. The luridly, warlike cavalcade proceeded at once to General Brooke's spacious headquarters in the agency residence. At a given signal all leaped to the ground, hitched their ponies to the trees, and guided by Father Jute, they entered the General's apartments, where the council was held, lasting two hours.

At the beginning of the pow-wow General Brooke explained that the Great Father, through him, asked them to come in and have a talk regarding the situation. A great deal of misunderstanding and trouble had arisen by the reports taken to and fro between the camps by irresponsible parties, and it was, therefore, considered very necessary that they have a talk face to face.

Through him, he said, the Father wanted to tell them if they would come in near the agency where he (Gen. Brooke) could see them often and not be compelled to depend on heresay, that he would give them plenty to eat and employ many of their young men as scouts, etc. He said he had heard they were hostile Indians, but he did not believe it. The soldiers did not come there to fight, but to protect the settlers and keep peace. He hoped they (the Indians) were all in favor of peace as the Great Father did not want war. As to the feeling over the change in the boundary line between Pine Ridge and the Rosebud Agency, he said that and many other things would be settled satisfactorily after they had shown a disposition to come in as asked by the Great Father. Wounded Knee was suggested as a place that would prove satisfactory to the Great Father to have them live. The representatives of the hostiles listened with contracted brows, sidelong glances at one another and low grunts.

When the General had concluded his remarks, Turning Bear came forward and spoke in reply.

"It would be a bad thing for them to come nearer the agency because there was no water or grass for their horses there. He could not understand how their young men could be employed as scouts if there was no enemy to be watched. They would be glad to be employed and get paid for it. They might come in, but as the old men and old women have no horses, and as their people have nothing generally to pull their wagons, it would take them a long time to come.

If they should come they would want the Great Father to send horses and wagons out to the Bad Land camp and bring in the great quantity of beef, etc., they had there, and take it anywhere to a new camp that might be agreed on. In conclusion the speaker hoped that they would be given something to eat before they started back."

To this the General replied that they should be given food. As for horses and wagons being sent after the beef, the General said that and many other things would be considered after they had acceded to the Great Father's request to move into the agency. Any reference whatever to the wholesale devastation and depredation, thieving and burning of buildings, etc., was studiously avoided on both sides. After the pow-wow was over, the band was conducted to the Quartermaster's Department and there given a big feast. The squaws living at the agency came out in gala day feathers and gave a squaw dance.

The dispatches of December 10th ran in brief, as follows:

Indications at General Miles's headquarters to-day pointed to a dramatic close of the Messiah craze among the Indians of the Northwest. An immediate tightening of the great military cordon now completely surrounding the ghost dancers seems to be the programme.

The climax apparently will be a total disarming of the redskins enclosed like so many rats in a huge trap. General Brooke is on the south, Colonel Sumner is on the north, General Carr is on the west and Colonel Merriam is on the east with their respective commands.

Those of the 11th ran thus:

Reports from General Ruger and General Brooke are quite favorable. The presence of the troops now in position has had a demoralizing influence upon the Indians, and those that a week ago were defiant and warlike are now giving evidence of submission. General Brooke reports that the Indians near White River have turned loose their stolen stock and were coming in. Colonel Sumner reports quite a large number of Indians in his vicinity who are willing to obey his orders. These belong to Big Foot's followers and others, located about the southwestern part of Cheyenne River.

On the 12th General Brooke reported from Pine Ridge:

From reports received I am of the opinion that Two Strike and all the other chiefs are coming in from White River. Short Bull and Kicking Bear, with a small following, broke away and went back into the Bad Lands. Think it likely they will go north; I have notified all troops north and west. There was quite a fight, and some Indians were hurt. I shall try to get them in here, but they may get beyond reach.

The Indians in the "Bad Lands" had fallen out among themselves over the question of returning to the agency, and a terrible battle ensued at Grass Basin between the followers of Short Bull and Two Strike, in which the latter triumphed. A battle also took place between the Indians and settlers on French Creek, in which the Indians were worsted.

In pursuance of the plan to use the Indian police for the purpose of arresting Ghost Dancers and those who refused to come into the agencies, General Miles sent out a strong squad to the headquarters of Sitting Bull, on the Grand River, with orders to prevent his escape into the Bad Lands as was his declared intention. This wily and powerful Chief, whose influence over the Sioux and their neighbors had never ceased to be a source of trouble, might have prolonged the agitation indefinitely, or precipitated bloody hostilities, had he been allowed to escape. It was therefore important to arrest him, and the attempt to do so led to his death. It was on December 15, that the Indian police started out to arrest Sitting Bull, having understood that he proposed starting for the Bad Lands at once.

The police were followed by a troop of cavalry under Captain Fouchet and infantry under Colonel Drum. When the police reached Sitting Bull's camp on the Grand River, about forty miles from Standing Rock, they found arrangements being made for departure. The cavalry had not yet reached the camp when the police arrested Bull and started back with him. His followers attempted his rescue and fighting commenced. Four policemen were killed and three wounded. Eight Indians were killed, including Sitting Bull and his son, Crow Foot and several others wounded.

The police were surrounded for some time, but maintained their ground until relieved by United States troops, who took possession of Sitting Bull's camp, with all women, children and property. Sitting Bull's followers, probably one hundred men, deserted their families and fled west up the Grand River.

General Schofield when asked for his opinion of the effect on the other Indians of the killing of Sitting Bull, said, "He indulged the hope expressed by others that this would hasten the settlement of the Indian trouble. He thought it would make more definite the lines of division between the friendly Indians and those determined to be hostile. He had from the start of the trouble in the Northwest, hoped the matter would be settled, without conflict, and regretted that blood had been shed, but he hoped for favorable results."

When Secretary Proctor was asked concerning the effect of the killing he said he did not think it would have any bad effect on friendly Indians. They had not been kindly disposed towards Sitting Bull, and had no love for him. It was only with the disaffected Indians that he had any influence.

When Sitting Bull surrendered to the United States authorities in the spring of '81, he was at first placed in the prison at Fort Randall, S. D., but later transferred to the Standing Rock Agency.

The old man felt the loss of his power keenly and sought some means to regain at least a part of his lost prestige.

Pretending that he desired to secure a farm and settle down like a white man, he was given a location on the beautiful Grand River, at a point 43 miles southwest of the Standing Rock Agency, which was located at a point half way between the Grand and Cannon Ball Rivers on the Missouri. At the home of Sitting Bull gathered a few who still acknowledged that he was a chief, and he longed for the time when he could again count over the large number of his followers,

During the time he was away from the agency, Gall, John Grass and other noted chiefs secured their former positions as leaders, and on Bull's return they were in a position to interfere with his ambition, and they thwarted his every move toward hostility to the Government, their influence with the Indians being so much greater than his, that they prevented much trouble that had been planned by the old rascal.

The first report of the coming of the Indian Messiah was hailed by Sitting Bull as the longed for opportunity, and he tried his best to take advantage of it.

Naturally superstitious, the Indians were ready for such an outpouring of their pent up feelings in the form of a religious dance. Bull had always gained his greatest success from his stability as a Medicine Man or diplomat, and he felt that the time for him to get his revenge on the other chiefs and the Government had arrived.

He at the start joined in with the ghost dancers, not shouting and dancing so much as inciting the others to the greater activity in that line.

When the Indians would go dancing around in a circle until they fell to the ground from dizziness and exhaustion, the wily old chief would take his place alongside of the fallen one, and, after a few words with him, would announce what visions the Messiah and the coming again of the hunting grounds of the past had been witnessed, and the dance would be resumed with renewed vigor. Soon another would fall in a faint and the same programme would be gone through with.

By carefully nursing this budding religious belief, Bull was fast regaining his old prestige, and it was but natural that the Government would, at the first announcement of his connection with the troubles, seek to effect his capture.

This had been planned at an early day by General Miles, but President Harrison thought the time had not yet come for such action and the arrest was postponed.

Buffalo Bill went out to Standing Rock Agency, with orders to bring Bull in, dead or alive, and he would have made a splendid attempt to do so had not the order been revoked.

Sitting Bull's followers after the death of their chief, fled up the Grand River, leaving behind them all their tools and their families, which were taken possession of by the soldiers.

After going a short distance up the river the fleeing redskins separated, and went off in all directions through the country towards the Bad Lands.

Colonel Corbin thus sketches Sitting Bull:

"The first time I saw Sitting Bull, was thirteen years ago. I was on a commission with General Terry and we met him near Fort Walsh. He was then about 40 years of age. He has never been a chief nor even a warrior of a high order. In the Custer massacre and in the fight with Reno he skipped out with his people and got away from danger. He has been a leader in organizing the Ghost Dance and has taken advantage of the religious craze to send emissaries to different bands to induce them to make trouble. The purpose was to assemble the warriors in the spring and with the aid of the Messiah bring back to life all of the dead Indians and restore the country to all its pristine glory. Sitting Bull was a shrewd politician and took advantage of the prevalent sentimental feeling.

He took his children out of school and gathered about him the small band he had in this secluded place, where he believed he would not be disturbed. It was necessary to take steps to arrest him."

General Miles thus viewed the situation:

"My information was reliable and positive of his (Sitting Bull's) emissaries and runners going to different tribes and exciting them to hostility, and of the reports in returning to his camp. The order for his arrest was not given any too soon, as he was about leaving the reservation with 100 fighting men.

The effect of his death has been disheartening to many others. I have directed the troops to ride down and capture or destroy the few that have escaped after his death from Standing Rock. General Brooke has more than 1000 lodges, or 5000 Indians, under his control at Pine Ridge, but there are still 50 lodges or over 200 fighting men in the Bad Lands that are very defiant and hostile."

On December 17, General Brooke reported that Two Strike and 184 lodges with 800 Indians had come in, and were encamped in front of the agency at Pine Ridge. A great number still remained in the Bad Lands, defiant and threatening war. Every possible means were being used to restrain the friendly Sioux then on the reservation. Their number was estimated at 16,000.

On the 18th, skirmishes were reported at a ranche near Smithville. A constant watch was kept over the movements in the Bad Lands. Accounts of depredations and murders were constantly coming to the respective headquarters.

On December 20th, 500 friendlies left Pine Ridge for the Bad Lands to urge the hostiles to come in. 39 of Sitting Bull's followers sent word that they would return. This was regarded as most favorable news. Big Foot and Stump surrendered and returned to the agency. General Miles had all his troops well in hand, and the cordon was so tight that none of the hostiles could escape, not even through the intricate passages of the Bad Lands. He was hopeful of a general surrender at no distant day. Official data showed the following mortality in the attempt to arrest Sitting Bull:— .

"Police Force—Bull Head, in command, dangerously wounded (four wounds); Shave Head, First Sergeant, mortally wounded (since dead); Little Eagle, Fourth Sergeant, killed; Middle, private, painfully wounded; Afraid of Soldier, private, killed; John Armstrong, special police, killed; Hawkman, special police, killed.

"Hostiles—Killed outright, Sitting Bull, Black Bird, Catch the Bear, Little Assinaboine, Crow Foot, (Sitting Bull's son, 17 years old). (The above are designated as very bad men.) Spotted Horn Bull, a chief; Brave Thunder, a chief, and Chase, wounded. Several were badly wounded, but were carried off by their friends.

On December 25, word came from Fort Bennett that the Indian war there was over. It seemed that the Indians there were worse scared than anybody, and would have come in long before, but for the fact that they feared massacre. After the Indians arrived at Bennett several councils of war were held to determine whether they would give up their arms or not. Finally they agreed to when General Miles asked them. Agent Palmer said: "No arms, no rations or blankets." This soon brought them to time, and all arms were soon stacked at the agency. Captain Hearst, commanding officer at Fort Sully, received the capitulation of 174 Uncapapas, including 70 of Sitting Bull's band and 30 from Rosebud Agency. Narcisse Narcelle, boss farmer, brought in 412 of Big Foot's Indians. Out of these 98 stands of arms were collected. They were nearly all Winchesters, of every description and of very antiquated pattern.

Sitting Bull's men wanted to remain at Cheyenne, and said they are afraid to return to Standing Rock. All surrendered, and the best of care was given them. All of the teams at the agency were started to Dupree, to bring in the sick women and children. Many of the leaders among the Indians acted very ugly in making final settlements, and there was a great deal of quarreling among themselves.

Two attempts were made by hostiles to break up a camp of Cheyenne scouts on Battle Creek. The first attack was made by only a few of the Indians, who were quickly repulsed, with a loss of two killed and several wounded. Three of the Cheyenne Indian scouts were wounded, and it is thought one is fatally hurt.

The second attack was made after dark by what was supposed to be the whole band, who were led by Kicking Bear himself. Volley after volley was fired on both sides, and a desultory fire was kept up for an hour or more.

On December 28, General Miles received word of the success of the friendly commission sent into the Bad Lands. "The hostiles there," says the dispatch, "had listened to the persuasion of General Brooke's Ogalalla and Brule peace commissioners, and were moving in toward Pine Ridge. This confirmed by General Brooke's dispatches yesterday. The whole body of braves, squaws, and papooses of the Brules, Cheyennes and Northern Indians who have been enjoying several weeks' outing at the famous terrace of Wall Camps in the Bad Lands, killing and smoking beef, stealing horses and engaging in other healthful and exciting pastimes, are now *en route* to the hospitable agency at Pine Ridge.

General Miles has issued orders to General Carr, Colonel Ofell and Captain Ford, in command of the western and northern sections of the cordon, to send in forces to carefully search the Bad Lands for straggling Indians, cached arms, etc., and to draw in toward the agency.

It seems that Big Foot had made his escape from the agency after his surrender, and had succeeded in eluding pursuit. But his camp was now found near Wounded Knee, by General Forsyth's command, and he determined to disarm it at once. He, (December 29th,) issued orders to have the 150 male Indians, who had been prisoners called from the tepees, saying he wanted to talk to them. They obeyed slowly and sullenly, and ranged in a semi-circle in front of the tent where Big Foot, their chief, lay sick with pneumonia. By twenties they were ordered to give up their arms. The first twenty went to their tents and came back with only two guns.

This irritated Major Whiteside, who was superintending this part of the work. After a hasty consultation with General Forsyth he gave the order for the cavalrymen, who were all dismounted and formed in almost a square about 25 paces back, to close in. They did so and took a stand within 20 feet of the Indians, now in their centre. When this was done a detachment of cavalrymen afoot was sent to search the tepees.

This work had hardly been entered upon when the 120 desperate Indians turned upon the soldiers who were gathered closely about the tepees, and immediately a storm of firing was poured upon the military.

It was as though the order to search had been the signal. The soldiers, not anticipating any such action, had been gathered in very closely, and the first firing was terribly disastrous to them. The reply was immediate, however, and in an instant it seemed that the draw in which the Indian camp was set, was a sunken Vesuvius. The soldiers, maddened at the sight of their falling comrades, hardly awaited the command, and in a moment the whole front was a sheet of fire, above which the smoke rolled, obscuring the central scene from view.

Through this horrible curtain single Indians could be seen at times flying before the fire, but after the first discharge from the carbines of the troopers there were few of them left; they fell on all sides like grain in the course of the scythe. Indians and soldiers lay together, and wounded fought on the ground. Off through the draw toward the bluffs the few remaining warriors fled. Turning occasionally to fire, but now evidently caring more for escape than battle. Only the wounded Indians seemed possessed of the courage of devils. From the ground where they had fallen they continued to fire until their ammunition was gone or until killed by the soldiers.

Both sides forgot everything, excepting only the loading and discharging of arms. It was only in the early part of the affray that hand to hand fighting was seen. The carbines were clubs, sabres gleamed, and war clubs, circling in the air, came down like thunder bolts. But this was only for a short time. The Indians could not stand that storm from the soldiers—they had not hoped to. It was only a stroke of life before death. The remnant fled, and the battle became a hunt. It was now that the artillery was called into requisition. Before, the fighting was so close that the guns could not be trained without danger of death to the soldiers. Now, with the Indians flying where they might, it was easier to reach them. The Gatling and Hotchkiss guns were trained, and then began a heavy firing which lasted half an hour, with frequent heavy volleys of musketry and cannon.

It was a war of extermination now with the troopers and it was difficult to restrain the troops. The tactics were almost abandoned. About the only tactics were to kill while it could be done. Wherever an Indian could be seen, down into the creek and up over the bare hills they were followed by artillery and musketry fire, and for several minutes the engagement went on, until not a live Indian was in sight.

On December 30, the following official telegrams passed:

The losses in this sudden affair were, Captain Wallace, 7th Cavalry, and 25 men killed; Lieutenant Garlington and 34 men wounded; also Lieutenant Hawthorne, 2d Cavalry, and 150 Indians killed, wounded and captured. The news of the battle at Wounded Knee excited the Indians at Pine Ridge in an alarming manner. The entire camp was soon in commotion, and the restless young bucks at once took to the hills, apparently eager for the fray. Even the most loyal of the Indians were affected, and the couriers themselves seemed eager for blood. It was not long before desultory firing was heard near the agency.

254 MASTERING THE SITUATION.

General Brook telegraphed as follows :

Colonel Forsyth says 62 dead Indian men were counted on the plain where the attempt was made to disarm Big Foot's band and where the fight begun; on other parts of the ground there where 18 more. These did not include those killed in ravines, where dead warriors were seen but not counted. Six were brought in badly wounded and six others were with a party of 23 men and women, which Captain Jackson had to abandon when attacked by about 160 Brule Indians from the agency. This accounts for 92 men killed and leaves but few alive and unhurt. The women and children broke for the hills when the fight commenced and comparatively few of them were hurt and few brought in. 39 are here, of which number, 21 are wounded. Had it not been for the attack by the Brules an accurate account would have been made, but the ravines were not searched afterwards. I think this shows very little apprehension from Big Foot's band in the future. A party of 40 is reported as held by the scouts at the head of Mexican Creek. These consist of all sizes, and the cavalry from Rosebud will bring them in if it is true.

JOHN R. BROOKE.

These Indians under Big Foot were among the most desperate there were; 38 of the remainder

MASTERING THE SITUATION. 255

of Sitting Bull's following that joined Big Foot on the Cheyenne river, and 30 that broke away from Hump's following, when he took his band and Sitting Bull's Indians to Fort Bennett, making in all, nearly 160 warriors. Before leaving their camps on the Fort Cheyenne River they cut up their harness, mutilated their wagons, and started South for the Bad Lands, evidently intending not to return, but to go to war. Troops were placed between them and the Bad Lands, and they never succeeded in joining the hostiles there. All their movements were intercepted, and their severe loss at the hands of the Seventh Cavalry, may be a wholesome lesson to the other Sioux.

MILES.

General Schofield said that the fight was a most unfortunate occurrence, but that he did not see how it could have been avoided. He sent a telegram to General Miles saying that he regarded the news received from him as still encouraging, and expressing an opinion that he (Miles) would be master of the situation very soon. He also expressed his thanks to the officers and men of the Seventh Cavalry for the gallant conduct displayed by them.

This fight gave rise to a remarkable diversity of sentiment among army officers and civilians. The slaughter of women and children, a thing so unusual in civilized warfare, called for an explanation and defence. General Forsyth was placed under duress and a commission was ordered to inquire into the fact whether he had been guilty of conduct unbecoming an officer. The moral effect of his victory was lost in the suspicions which clouded it. The Commissioner of Indian affairs wrote to the Supervisor of Education at Pine Ridge for his opinion of the battle. His reply, in brief, was:

The testimony of the survivors of Big Foot's band is unanimous on one important point—namely, that the Indians did not deliberately plan a resistance. The party was not a war party, according to their statements (which I believe to be true), but a party intending to visit the agency at the invitation of Red Cloud.

The Indians say that many of the men were unarmed. When they sent the troops they anticipated no trouble. There was constant friendly intercourse between the soldiers and the Indians, even women shaking hands with the officers and men. The demand for their arms was a surprise to the Indians, but the great majority of them chose to submit quietly. The tepees had already been searched, and a large number of guns, knives and hatchets confiscated when the searching of the persons of the men was begun.

The women say that they too were searched, and their knives (which they always carried for domestic purposes) taken from them. A number of the men had surrendered their rifles and cartridge belts, when one young man (who is described by the Indians as a good-for-nothing young fellow) fired a single shot. This called forth a volley from the troops, and the firing and confusion became general.

I do not credit the statement, which has been made by some, that the women carried arms and participated actively in the fight. The weight of testimony is overwhelmingly against this supposition. There may have been one or two isolated cases of this kind, but there is no doubt that the great majority of the women and children, as well as many unarmed men and youth, had no thought of anything but flight. They were pursued up the ravines and shot down indiscriminately by the soldiers.

It is reported that one of the officers called out, "Don't shoot the squaws," but the men were doubtless too much excited to obey. The killing of the women and children was in part unavoidable, owing to the confusion, but I think there is no doubt that it was in many cases deliberate and intentional. The 7th Cavalry, Custer's old command, had an old grudge to repay.

The party of scouts who buried the dead report eighty-four bodies of men and boys, forty-four of women, and eighteen of young children. Some were carried off by the hostiles. A number of prisoners, chiefly women, have since died of their wounds, and more will soon follow. The party who visited the battlefield on January 1 to rescue any wounded who might have been abandoned, and brought in seven, report that nearly all the bodies of the men were lying close about Big Foot's tents, while the women and children were scattered along a distance of two miles from the scene of the encounter.

The main reflection which occurs to me in connection with this most important affair, is that the same thing should not be allowed to happen again. The irresponsible action of one hot headed youth should not be the signal for a general and indiscriminate slaughter of the unarmed and helpless.

The battle of Wounded Knee was followed by an attack on the Catholic Mission at Clay Creek. The dispatches from Pine Ridge respecting this affair, read as follows :

The Seventh Cavalry had just reached camp yesterday morning, (Dec. 30th.) after repulsing the attack made on their supply train by Two Strike's band, when a courier arrived with word that the Catholic mission was on fire and the teachers and pupils were being massacred. In 20 minutes the weary and hungry and almost exhausted cavalry were once more in motion. They found that the fire was at the day school one mile this side of the mission.

The Indians, under command of Little Wound and Two Strike, were found to the number of 1809 about a mile beyond the Mission. The Seventh formed a line and began the fighting, which was carried on by only 30 or 40 Indians at a time, while the great mass kept concealed. General Forsyth suspected an ambush and did not let them draw him into dangerous ground. Colonel Henry started one hour later than Forsyth, and, owing to the exhaustion of his horses, had to travel very slow. The Seventh became surrounded by the redskins, but just as the circle was ready to charge, the Ninth broke in upon the rear of the hostiles and they vanished. The weary soldiers slowly retreated, reaching the agency at dark. The infantry had been ordered out, but were stopped by the sight of the head of the column of cavalry. The soldiers, heroic and brave as they were, were greatly outnumbered, and there are not enough troops at this point to clean out these Indians, who are still camped within seven miles of the agency. The damage sustained by the troops is small. Lieutenant

Mann, of Company E, Seventh Cavalry, was wounded, shot through the side. The First Sergeant of Company K was also wounded.

The situation was exceedingly gloomy in every respect. The weather became intensely cold. Blinding snow storms were raging. Bands of hostiles renewed their depredations all along the Nebraska and Dakota border, and the militia of the former State was called into service. General Miles took the field in person and started from Chadwick to Pine Ridge at the head of a large force of cavalry. Rumors were constantly arriving to hand, of the breaking away of the Indians from the agency for the purpose of joining the hostiles in the Bad Lands. Only squaws and those unable to fight remained behind to draw rations and keep up a show of friendliness. One of the most useful of the missionaries, Father Craft, received severe wounds in the indiscriminate firing around Pine Ridge. Sentiment seemed to shape up everywhere that a slaughter was imminent, and that nothing but an exterminating warfare would meet the situation.

The dispatches of January 1, 1891, dated at Pine Ridge ran as follows:

The upper Brules are in open rebellion. After two months of unrest and uncertainty the Sioux have finally shown their hand. Three thousand of them, under the leadership of such cunning fellows as Big Road, Kicking Bear, Little Wound, Short Bull and Jack Red Cloud, and even old Red Cloud himself, have turned upon the Government, for what will doubtless prove to be their last stand against the military. American Horse is the only remaining loyal chief, but his following is so small that it would make no difference whether he counseled war or peace.

Squads of Indians have been leaving for the warpath to-day. Under the cloak of a heavy snow storm, they started off to the north, but their destination is not known. It is thought, however, that they will make for the Bad Lands, or the vicinity of the old Spotted Tail reservation. Troops have been ordered to intercept them. Depredations have already begun on the ranches. Scores of houses along White River have been burned and the cattle run off and killed.

A scout, who came in Tuesday night, said that the hostiles, reassured by the fact that the soldiers quit the field during the afternoon, had planned to attack and burn the agency with fire-arrows, then stampede the troops and massacre the inhabitants. The report was true to some extent, but the heavy lines of pickets stopped the savages.

General Brooke ordered 100,000 rounds of ammunition from Omaha.

The panic in the railroad towns in the vicinity of Pine Ridge was indescribable. Settlers were pouring into the villages on foot, in wagons and on horseback. Many of them abandoned their stock and household goods, while others brought their cattle and ponies with them. Some of the refugees who traveled through the blizzard were badly frozen, and many women and children became ill from exposure.

On the morning of January 2d, 1891, General Miles telegraphed General Schofield, saying that 3,000 Indians, men, women and children, and including about 600 bucks, are now encamped in a section of the Bad Lands, about fifteen miles from the Pine Ridge agency, and that there is almost a cordon of troops around them. General Miles announces that he hopes to be able to induce these hostiles to surrender without a struggle. The spot where they are encamped he describes as somewhat like the lava beds of California, where the Modocs made their final fight. It is an excellent position from an Indian standpoint, but there are no avenues of escape, all having been closed by the troops. General Miles says the Indians have gathered some cattle and provisions, and appear to be determined to make their fight for supremacy at this point. He says he will make another effort to get them back to the agency without bloodshed, and, in order to do so, he has established a regular siege around this stronghold.

The forces at his command at this date were the First, Sixth, Seventh (eight companies), and Ninth Cavalry; one company of the First Artillery, Company E; one company of the Fourth Artillery, Company F; and the First, Second, Third, Seventh, Eighth, Twelfth, Sixteenth, Seventeenth, Twentieth, Twenty-first, Twenty-second and Twenty-fifth Infantry, making in all 151 companies. This should have meant an actual fighting force of at least 10,000 officers and men, but it is probable that the ranks were not full, and that the regular army under General Miles did not exceed 8,000 men at the most.

While every day brought his forces more and more in touch, there could be no doubt of the fact that the hostiles in the Bad Lands were being augmented by desertions from the agencies, and their leaders such as Short Bull, Two Strike and probably Red Cloud (though the latter was credited being in the employ of the Government), were very determined upon war. But while this was so, there was a large contingent of those who ranked as hostiles which favored peaceful return to the agencies. The hostiles, therefore, were discordant, and time would only widen the sources of discontent. The excitement attending and following the Wounded Knee affair, had interfered with the getting of accurate information, but General Miles persisted in a quiet and resolute movement of his forces toward the hostile centres. Old Red Cloud came on January 8th, and reported that he had lost all control over the younger men of his tribe.

The nearness of the troops to the hostiles was attended with its dangers. Skirmishes were not infrequent. Scouting parties hardly knew what moment they might be the victims of ambush. On the line occupied by the 22d Infantry, almost incessant firing had been kept up for several days. On Jan. 7th, Lieutenant Casey was out with his scouts watching the hostile camp, and, with one Cheyenne, met two Indians, an Ogallalla and a Brule. The Ogallalla warned Lieutenant Casey that the Brules were bad, and would shoot. As Lieutenant Casey turned to go away the Brule fired, striking him in the back of the head and killing him instantly. Lieutenant Casey was one of the most brilliant and beloved officers of the service. He had been in command of a troop of Cheyenne scouts for about a year, and was working earnestly in the interest of the

Indians themselves. He had a reputation in the army of possessing an unusually accurate knowledge of the Indian character.

At this critical date the Interior Department of the Government summed up the situation as follows:

There are in all about 20,000 Sioux Indians, men, women and children, on the Northern reservations. Of this number 16,500 are accounted for, as they are living on the reservations in peace and not taking any part in the present disturbance. This leaves about 3,500 men, women and children to face the earthworks, the howitzers and the 8,000 men now under the command of General Miles. The hostile camp is located about 17 miles north of the agency, and the cordon of troops surrounds the hostile camp, with the exception of the south side, the object being to drive the Indians into the reservation. There is constant communication between the hostile camp and the agency. The hostiles are well supplied with beef, but they have no sugar or coffee, except as they are supplied by the "friendlies," as the reservation Indians are called. While the situation is regarded as a hopeless one for the Indians, yet it is believed that they have no intention of surrendering.

At this juncture the Government deemed it wise to transfer the agencies from the Interior to the War Department. General Miles regarded this as an excellent move. It avoided conflict of authority and left him unmolested in his policy of slowly drawing his cordon around the hostiles, avoiding bloodshed, unless it became inevitable, giving them time to get over their craze and return to reason. He was convinced that dissensions among the hostiles were daily growing, and that he could afford to wait, so long as they were destroying one another.

At intervals of every two or three days, he ordered his troops to take up advanced positions, a few miles nearer the hostile camps. These movements were generally made under cover of the night, and the following morning would reveal the unwelcome truth to the hostiles that their case was hourly growing more and more desperate. Moreover, proximity gave those who wished to come in a chance to do so, for they could reach the cover of the troops without the danger of pursuit.

By the 12th of December the policy of General Miles had begun to tell favorably on the hostiles. His show of force was such as to convince them of the futility of war on their part. Their dissensions, their lack of food, the passing away of the craze, the growth of the impression that after all the troops were not intended for their extermination, a gradual subsidence of all the thoughts and passions that had persuaded them—all these had had time to operate. The panicky feeling of the last few days was passing away, and the beginning of a peaceful end was believed to be in sight.

This feeling was confirmed by news that prominent chiefs were relenting and were anxious to come within the protection of the agency. Soon came other news to the effect that they were actually moving toward the agency with their followers. While they had to be watched as enimies, for there was no telling whether they were acting in good faith or not, they were nevertheless encouraged. Nothing was thrown in their way, on the contrary, they were permitted to move just as fast as they saw fit, the thought being that the more voluntary their surrender the more effective it would be. Gentle pressure was exerted behind in the shape of a closing in of the troops. The scene about Pine Ridge grew animated. The effect of the coming of the hostiles on those already within the agency was watched with interest, not to say apprehension. Every point available for strategy had been fortified and occupied, so that if the hostiles should infect the friendlies or should choose to break their faith, they could be punished in a summary manner.

General Miles was now in a position to make the demand on those who came in, that a condition of their surrender, should be a giving up of their arms. This hardest of all conditions for an Indian, was sternly resented at first, but as the desperation of their situation became more and more apparent, it proved to be a condition to which they could concede, in their own way. That way was peculiar, but not unnatural. They secreted all their new and available arms, and very complacently began to turn in their old and useless weapons. The trick was not resented, for the time at least, the great point being to get a surrender. As long as the arms were not in hand, but cached in some out of the way place, the Indians would be as good as disarmed. The situation as shown by the dispatches of the 12th. of December was thus:

The announcement that a large number of the hostiles had at length arrived within gunshot distance of the pickets spread with rapidity through the camp of the Indians near the camp fire. Immediately hundreds of squaws and children gathered in the vicinity of headquarters, whence a view of the bluffs beyond upon which the hostiles were stationed could be obtained.

They waited patiently for their brothers, lovers and husbands to appear, but as evening drew on and their devotion was not rewarded, they gradually retired to their tepees.

At this writing there is no certainty as to what the Indians will do. General Miles himself is in doubt as to what to expect then. They may, he says, get within gunshot of the agency, and then break away to the camp which they have just abandoned. Fear of all kinds of punishment seems to have taken possession of them, and it is generally understood that one injudicious act on the part of the soldiers, or the mad act of some implacable hostile would precipitate a fight, the consequence of which may be scarcely imagined.

Captain Ewers will start in a few days with Little Chief's band of 490 Cheyennes to take them to the Tongue River, Montana. Little Chief and his band have been ugly fighters in every war for the last twenty years. In 1876 they were sent from this region to Fort Reno, and in 1878 fought their way back through the settlements of Kansas, and Nebraska, to the Sand Hills, near Gordon, where they were captured. Since then they have been good friends to the whites, and have made excellent police and scouts. The band have about 900 relatives on the Tongue river, and have begged for several years to be transferred to the reservation.

General Miles determined this morning not to parley nor confer again with the Indians, and this morning he sent a messenger to the hostiles camped at the Mission, stating his terms. He said they must come into the Agency in small squads, and go into camp on their grounds near the friendly Indians. He would not object if they choose their own camping grounds, but the Brules and Ogallallas must not camp together, and they must submit to the laws governing the reservation and to the agent.

The Indians themselves partially admit the chiefs cannot guarantee to control the warriors. They say they have among them about 300 young bucks who want to fight, and a single shot will start them. Besides this, the Indians who murdered Lieutenant Casey are known, and they know when they are taken they will be hanged for murder. They are among the belligerent young bucks, and they may precipitate a fight to prevent dying by the rope. There are all these possibilities which make it impossible to predict the result. General Miles is required to exercise patience almost to a ridiculous degree. He has given the matter already more time than there is any earthly reason for. If an attack is made, a cry will go up from the Indians that they were bringing in their wounded; that their squaws had no ponies, and that they were not given time to come in. It is well understood here what the effect of this complaint would be in the East, and so General Miles is compelled to wait and let the Indians suit themselves, and move back and forth at their pleasure. Some of them came to the Mission, six miles northwest of here, Saturday night. Scouts reported that all the hostiles were there and they would be in Sunday morning. Double guards were put out, lights were kept in the tents all night, and every man slept with his arms within reach. In the morning word came that the band which had been at the Mission the night before had returned to the main body, 15 miles away, and that they were almost in. The hostiles have runners out, and they have been in the camp of the "friendlies" for the last 24 hours, trying to get into the military camp. The Indians are just as anxious to know what the whites are going to do as the whites are to know what the Indians will do.

Shortly after noon it was discovered that the hostiles had made a rapid advance, and about 1,000 of them had arrived to within 1,000 yards of the pickets outside the agency. General Miles and staff went to the picket lines, and after a short inspection of the bands, returned to the agency for the time being.

The Indians will not be permitted to enter the agency, and communication with them from within has been prohibited. When they do come in the Ogallalla Sioux will be stationed near Red Cloud's house west of the agency, while the Brules will be placed on the east. On the same day General Miles wrote to Buffalo Bill that the hostiles were within half a mile of the agency and that nothing but an accident could prevent the establishment of peace. He authorized the withdrawal of the State troops and thanked them for the confidence they had afforded the people in their frontier homes.

Though between three and four hundred of the hostiles broke away from their camp near the agency, on the morning of January 13th, and made their escape to the Bad Lands, the remainder clung to their resolution to come in, and their camp was in full view of the agency fortifications. The view from the fortifications was grandly picturesque. Behind them was a natural amphitheatre. A rugged broken slope two hundred feet to the crest. It was just a mile from the agency, and White Clay creek runs beside it. On the plain were tepees by the hundred, pitched irregularly, huddled together in groups here and scattered widely apart there. Moving about among the tepees a field glass showed the bucks and squaws with their children and dogs. Such a spectacle imprinted itself on the mind with startling clearness, for it was huge in its grandeur, strikingly unique and wonderfully suggestive to the imagination.

Just between the plain and the agency, perched on a hill behind earthworks, was a three-inch rifle, which was trained on the camp. It seemed to stare grimly down on the village of half-crazed barbarians and to warn them of the awful horror that would follow one rash act.

General Miles sent the following to General Schofield :—

"General Brooke's command is now camped five miles distant on White Clay Creek, and the entire body of Indians are between the two commands. General Brooke has commanded his force with considerable skill and excellent judgment. The greatest difficulty is now to restore confidence. The Indians have great fear that arms will be taken away, and then all treated like those who were on Wounded Knee They have a large number of wounded women and children, which creates a most depressing feeling among the families, and a desperate disposition among them. Military measures and movements have been successful. The control and government now becomes the problem, yet no serious embarrassment is apprehended at present."

By January 15th the situation had much improved. The dispatches ran thus:—

"The Indians have at last come, or, rather are coming in. They string along the west bank of the White Clay Creek for a distance of two miles. They are mounted, walking, riding on wagons, and, in fact, are advancing in every manner known to them. They are driving and leading immense herds of ponies. Some of them are entering the friendlies' camp; others are pitching their tepees on the west bank of the White Clay. These are the Ogallallas. The Brules, however, are camping in the bottom, around Red Cloud's house, and half a mile from the agency buildings.

The number of lodges is estimated at 742, and the number of Indians cannot be fewer than 3,500. General Brooke has been ordered to march with his command from below the mission to this point and will reach here to-day. A part of his command will camp on the west bank of White Clay, extending north of the Indians, while another will flank them on the west and south. The advance guard of the hostiles had scarcely reached the agency when Big Road sent word that he had collected the arms of his followers and wanted to surrender them to the agency. When the weapons came in they were found to consist of simply two shot-guns, a heavy rifle and a broken carbine, two Sharp's rifles and one Winchester—nine guns in all.

This surrender is an evidence that the Indians do not propose to give up all their guns and that they have hidden their best weapons in the hills. Standing Bear, American Horse, White Bird and Spotted Horse, friendly chiefs, are now asking protection from the hostiles, who have camped among them."

Official dispatches from General Miles to General Schofield contained the following:—

"In order to restore entire confidence among these Indians, I have found it necessary to send a delegation to Washington, to receive assurance of the highest authority of the good intentions of the Government toward them. This will answer a double purpose, namely, satisfy them, bridge over the transition period between war and peace, dispel distrust and hostility, and restore confidence. It will also be a guarantee of peace while they are absent. I ask that my action may receive the approval of the Department by telegraph. Everything is progressing satisfactorily, and I can see no reason why perfect peace may not be established."

The reply from Schofield was:—

"The Secretary of War conferred with the President and the Secretary of the Interior, in regard to your proposal to send a delegation of the Sioux Chiefs to Washington, and they approve of your recommendation.

The Secretary of the Interior has sent an agent to conduct them. It is desired that the delegation be as small as possible, five or six, or not more than ten. If the delegation has already started, telegraph at once the number, route and commanding officer."

On the same date, January 15th, 1891, General Miles telegraphed to Schofield, announcing the end of Indian troubles in the west. "The entire camp of Indians," says Miles, "came into the agency this morning. They moved in three columns while passing under the guns of the command."

General Miles thought it fair to estimate their number at not less than 4,000 people. He says he has directed the chiefs to have the different bands gather up their arms and turn them in, which they were doing. He continues:

"Kicking Bear, supposed to be the leader, was the first to surrender his rifle this morning, and others of the same character will follow his example. Of course, many of the young men may hold back and may cache their arms, but I believe the disarming will be complete. Both officers and men have exercised and maintained a most commendable discipline, patience and fortitude. All are gratified with the result. It will require some time to get the Indians under full control, but everything is moving in a satisfactory manner. The troops under General Brooke have moved forward and are now in three strong commands, with the Indians, upward of 7,000, in the centre, the whole within the radius of ten miles."

In reply to the telegram sent by General Schofield concerning the departure of the Indian delegation for Washington, General Miles says: "There is no necessity of haste. I do not intend to send delegation until this matter is entirely settled here, and Indians do as I have directed, which directions they are now complying with in every respect. This Indian war I now consider at an end in the most satisfactory manner. A more complete submission to the military power has never been known."

'The situation on Jan. 16th, 1891, was that 6,000 Indians still clung to their Winchesters with grim determination. "I must have them," said

General Miles, "even if it becomes necessary to pour a few wagon loads of lead into their camp in order to get them." He told the Chiefs that nothing short of a full surrender of arms would be accepted as an evidence of surrender. The Chiefs gave their word that every effort would be made to get the guns away from their followers, but every device was resorted to by the holders to avoid facing the music, while not a few positively refused to accept the terms offered. Miles remained firm and gave notice that all who did not give up their guns by night would have them taken away by force.

On the 17th, General Miles asked for a conference with the principal Chiefs. There was an immediate response. Among the Chiefs were Two Strikes, Short Bull, Eagle Pipe, Crow Dog, Big Turkey, Black Robe, Kicking Bear, Iron Foot and Man Raised Above. The Chiefs were Brules, and when the subject of returning to their agency at Rosebud was broached they said they were in favor of returning if a military man should be placed over them as agent.

After a little more parleying Big Road stood up and solemnly and dramatically proclaimed himself in favor of peace. At the same time he asked those who wished to join him in restoring peace and working for the prosperity of their people, to raise their right hand towards Heaven. Immediately every right hand in the gathering was raised on high, and, with a general shaking of hands, the conference came to a close.

On January 18th, the Secretary of the Interior (Secretary Noble), stated his views of the situation, now that he had been given to understand that the Indian trouble was practically over. First of all, he believed the Indians had no legitimate use for firearms, and, therefore, should be required to dispose of them.

Second, he thought that the intellect that could master the mechanical intricacies of the rifle was fully capable of comprehending and appreciating the usefulness and noble simplicity of the plow. He proposed to give the hostile Sioux an opportunity as well as an incentive to earn their own living. Of the 244,000 Indians in the United States, over two-thirds were earning their own living, and making material progress in civilization. The other third were depending largely, if not entirely, upon the Government for support. Of this latter class a large majority were Sioux, and they had become boastful, arrogant and dictatorial. They had been allowed to come to Washington every year or two, and had become deeply impressed with their own importance. Some of those who are most vehement in their demands that they continue to be fed and wholly maintained at the expense of the Government are the owners of quite large herds of cattle, from which they realize considerable sums of money. Nevertheless they insist, with much gusto, that the Government shall feed them, and when their rations are slightly reduced they daub on the paint and start out on the warpath. I am in favor, said the Secretary, of making these people work for their living, just as we white people are doing. They are strong, able-bodied men, of average intelligence, and there is no reason why they should not earn their bread. The Government has treated them with great generosity and consideration; especially is this true during the last half century. In the early days the settlers treated them as murderers of innocent men, women and children, and the insatiable enemies of the white race. Latterly they have beeen treated with more than kindness, and so they have come to believe that the white people are under never-ending obligations to them.

The time has fully come, in the opinion of the Secretary, when the hostile Sioux should be compelled to do something for their own support. They should be treated with perfect fairness and justice, but work should enter largely into any policy or scheme for their civilization.

By January 22nd, the submission of the hostiles had been so complete that General Miles resolved upon an honorary parade of his troops, the design being to celebrate the return of peace and to impress the Indians with the power of the Government, and a sense of their own weakness. Ten thousand Sioux were given an opportunity to view the strength and discipline of the force they had confronted. The day was one of the most disagreeable of the campaign. A furious wind blew from the north, driving sand and snow over the valley in blinding and choking sheets. The camp of the soldiers was two miles from the agency. Through a stifling gale of sand General Miles and his staff rode in a ragged group, the wind tossing the tails of their horses over their flanks. It was after 10 o'clock when all the preparations were complete for the review. The summits of the buttes to the north were then fringed with Sioux warriors, who were closely wrapped in their blankets and staring at the long lines of cavalrymen and infantry which stretched away to the south until they were lost in the flying sand. The redskins were still suspicious that some move would be made to wipe them off the face of the earth. Stretching in a long ghostly line along the ridge of the buttes to the north were their pickets ready to give the word that would send the redskins flying in case the soldiers should advance upon them.

General Miles sat upon his black horse on a knoll to the east in front of his escort. Finally there came through the gale the shrill notes of bugles. They were so faint that they were almost lost in the storm. Then one by one the troops took up the call and the great parade of the Regular Army began to pass in review. General Brooke, muffled up in a wolf skin overcoat, grimy from the sand that swirled about his horse, and followed by his staff, led the procession. When the horsemen passed in front of General Miles, the two leaders of the campaign tipped their hats, then General Brooke took a position beside his superior.

A cloud of sand now swept across the prairie, but through the blinding sheet, and with heads muffled in huge fur capes, came the great detachment of Sioux scouts with Captain Taylor, with his sword at a salute, at their head. Sergeant Redshirt, the handsomest Indian in the Sioux nation, was at the extreme right. Yankton Charlie, who saved the revolvers of poor Lieutenant Casey, rode at the left of the line, his overcoat buttoned so closely about him that the war feathers on his breast were concealed.

Behind these famous scouts was the First Regiment Band, of Angel Island, California, in fur mittens and caps, playing a march which was almost lost in the roar of the storm. Then came the great swinging column of infantry, in brown canvas overcoats, fur caps, and the glittering barrels of their rifles over their shoulders. Colonel Shafter rode at the head of the advance columns. The men marched in company front, with their red and white guidons tattered by shot and shell snapping spitefully in the gale. This was the famous First Regiment of the army, and as its officers passed in front of General Miles, their swords flashed through the flying sand and then fell at their saddle girths. The band now ceased playing, and in place of its melody there came the stirring and shrill mutterings of a dozen bugles. Behind the trumpeters tramped the Second Infantry, of Omaha, in blue overcoats and brown leggings, with Major Butler at their head; and then came the Seventeenth Infantry, swinging along with the jauntiness it displayed when it marched through the blizzard and sand along Cheyenne River.

There was a rumbling back of the Infantry where the mules were dragging the machine cannon. Those guns, the Indians declare, shoot to-day and kill to-morrow. Behind these machine cannon was Captain Capron's battery of three inch rifled guns, with soldiers holding their carbines and sitting on the caissons. Behind the artillery was General Carr, astride a bay horse and leading the Sixth Calvary, which has cut its way through the southwest from the Indian Nation to the Rio Grande. His entire regiment was prancing behind him, the troopers being muffled in canvas overcoats, with their rifles slung to their saddles. General Carr's hat went off with deliberate grace. Its response was the dipping of General Miles' sombrero. Then the famous leader of the southwestern troopers drew up alongside of General Miles and General Brooke, while his troops pushed forward through the storm. More Hotchkiss guns followed, and then came the Leavenworth battalion, a mixed regiment commanded by Colonel Sanford. Behind these troops was still another battery of Hotchkiss guns, the carriages of which still bore evidences of the furious storm of shot that raged for an hour at Wounded Knee.

A lean, shrunken face man, with his overcoat buttoned tightly around his throat, and mounted on a splendid horse, followed the cannon. It was Colonel Guy V. Henry, who was shot through the face in a battle with the Sioux, in 1876, and who led his flying negro troops of the 9th

Cavalry, in the all-night ride of 80 miles, to save the 7th Cavalry, which was threatened with Custer's fate at the Catholic Mission, less than four weeks ago. Behind him were long lines of black faces peering from fur caps and the high collars of buffalo overcoats. The negro Cavalry came in unbroken columns, with its world-famed and decorated heroes of the Thornburg massacre riding at the extreme left, and their carbines at a salute. Every man in the 9th Cavalry was in that long ebony wave of faces, and as it swept in front of General Miles, the famous Indian fighter dipped his hat again and again.

There was another battery of machine guns, and then came in long column front the most celebrated regiment in the Western Army. It was preceded by a bugle corps, mounted on white horses, and from the glittering instruments there came a roar that even the screaming of the storm could not drown. The troopers of the 7th Cavalry, a regiment that has been torn and leveled by the silent ghost dancers on the buttes, was approaching. The musicians from California began to play "Garryowen," a stirring, rollicking melody, which Custer said was fit music for any soldier's death. The troopers came with their carbines at a salute and their blue capes flung back, so that their yellow linings were exposed

Major Whiteside was in command of the regiment. As it passed General Miles, the whole staff doffed their hats, while the Commander himself waved his white-gloved hand. Troop after troop passed by with guidons that had been riddled by Indian bullets, until B troop and K troop came in view. The appearance of these troops aroused the emotions of the spectators. B troop was not so large as those that had preceded it, and K troop was even smaller. When the savages at Wounded Knee turned their carbines on the soldiers, these troops faced an awful fire. K troop was without its Commander and all of its commissioned and non-commissioned officers. The only officer to lead B troop was a second lieutenant, with a bandage about his head, but the gallant troopers who remained rode with a proud bearing. Their rifles were held over the heads of their horses. Behind the Cavalry came the hospital and supply trains and pack mules.

The column was an hour passing General Miles, their being nearly 4,000 soldiers and 3,700 horses and mules in line.

Such was the end of the Indian uprising of 1890-91, in the north-west. The promised Commission of Indian Chiefs came duly to Washington to consult with the "Great Father." They arrived about the last of January 1891, and were received, as all similar delegations have been, with impressive honors mingled with curiosity. They were shown around the Capital City to impress them with the exhaustless resources of the whites, and the beauty and comfort to be attained by our superior civilization. They were shown our arsenals, guns great and small, and our endless supplies of ammunition, as much as to say, "What General Miles has shown you at Pine Ridge is nothing to what we have in reserve for you if you do not behave yourselves." They were dined and wined to give them a good impression of our hospitality. About the time they were supposed to be in prime condition for an official reception by the "Great Father," another delegation of Chiefs came upon the scene, who claimed to be better representatives of the Sioux tribe and of the Indian situation, than the first. They proclaimed that the first delegation embraced only worthless Chiefs, who would not work and who were hostile at heart, whatever their professions might be. As this chapter closes, these rival delegations are urging their respective claims on the Government, with the prospect of exhausting the patience of the authorities, and achieving nothing of moment at last.

Chapter XIX.
SENTIMENT RESPECTING THE UPRISING.

AMID the sensationalism of the newspaper press and the prejudicial accounts of the Indian situation which go out from the agencies and the conflicting missionary centres one feels glad to strike a vein of candor. Such would seem to be found in the statements of Gen. Nelson A. Miles, who has not only mastered the recent critical situation, but who has been in contact with the Indians for a sufficiently long time to enable him to reason correctly and express himself intelligently and truthfully. He is the best situated man in the country to state impartially what he knows of the relation of the Red to the White race. That he has done so in his contribution to the *North American Review*, for January 1891, no one can have cause to doubt. We are so entirely convinced of the value of his views as to regard them as fitted for a permanent place in the history of Indian affairs, and as invaluable in the consideration of such a policy as will do credit to a powerful and advancing nation in its dealings with a weaker and receding nation. His conclusions, as given in very nearly his own language are as follows:—

The fact that we have had a few years of peace is no guarantee that it will continue. Within the last sixteen years we have had no less than nine Indian wars, and now we find ourselves threatened with a more serious and general uprising than any that has occurred during the whole history of Indian warfare. The confederation of the "Six Nations" by the prophet, the campaigns of Tecumseh, and the conspiracy of Pontiac did not extend over so vast an area of country, or embrace so many different tribes, many of whom have been hostile to each other, as the present conspiracy; and while the conditions are somewhat similar to those which have preceeded other Indian confederations, conspiracies and wars, this one has unusual features and causes.

The Indians are practically a doomed race, and none realize it better than themselves. They have contended inch by inch for every foot of territory from the Atlantic to the Pacific. The strength, superior intelligence and ingenuity of the white race in the construction of weapons of war, and their vast superiority in numbers, have not deterred the Indians from resisting the power of the whites and beginning hostilities, sometimes even with apparently little justification, cause or hope of success; and there would be nothing remarkable in the history of such a warlike people, if they made one desperate effort in the death-struggle of the race.

The subjugation of a race by their enemies cannot but create feelings of most intense hatred and animosity. Possibly if we should put ourselves in their place, we might comprehend their feelings. Suppose, for instance, that instead of being a nation of vast wealth, population, prosperity and happiness, our numbers were narrowed down to two hundred and fifty thousand souls, scattered in bands, villages or settlements of from five hundred to twenty thousand people, and confined within the limits of comparatively small districts. Suppose this vast continent had been overrun by sixty millions of people from Africa, India, or China, claiming that their civilization, customs, and beliefs were older and better than ours, compelling us to adopt their habits, language and religion, obliging us to wear the same style of raiment, cut our hair according to their fashion, live upon the same food, sing the same songs, worship the same Allahs, Vishnus and Brahmas; and we realized that such a conquest and the presence of such a horde of enemies had become a withering blight and a destroying scourge to our race: what then would be our feelings towards such a people? In considering this question we may be able to realize something of the feelings of the Indians to-day. They remember the romance of the freedom and independence they once enjoyed; the time when they could move from one pleasant valley to another; when they had all that an Indian desires, namely, plenty of food, comfortable lodges made of skins of the buffalo or elk, plenty of their kind of clothing; and when they were allowed to enjoy their customs, rites, and amusements, savage and brutal as they were.

The first time the writer met Sitting Bull was under a flag of truce between the lines, when he had a thousand warriors behind him; and during the conversation I think he expressed in a few words the true sentiment of the Indian. He was what might be considered a devotional man, frequently offering a little prayer and saluting the Great Spirit. One remark of his is certainly significant. Raising his eyes toward heaven, he said: "God Almighty made me an Indian, and he did not make me an agency Indian, and I do not intend to be one." That remark was indorsed by huge grunts of the stalwart savages within hearing, and it is **the sentiment of the** non-treaty, disaffected Indians **of** every tribe in every section of the great **West.** They prefer to be Indians in their wild and independent life rather than to be confined to the limits of any agency.

While we have continued the policy of using the military force of the government against **them** with all severity, **as soon** as that is completed and **the** tribes are **subjugated**, they are suddenly turned over to civilians, some from the far-off Eastern States, to try various experiments and to carry out the theories that they have of civilization. Take, for instance, the Kiowas, **Cheyennes and** Comanches **of the** Indian Territory. **Their** history has been a history of peace and **war** for many years. In 1874 they had a great convention or medicine-dance, which resulted in a general uprising, in which they became a terror to the whole southwest country. After committing many crimes and after many engagements with the troops, they were finally **worn down and** subjugated, and **surrendered with** scarcely any means **of continuing** hostilities. Most of the few remaining war ponies they had were sold; they gave up their pale and emaciated white captives, who **in turn** passed down the line of warriors and pointed out not less than seventy

Comanches who had committed horrible atrocities during the eight months of hostility. These seventy warriors were sent to Florida for punishment and the military control of the tribes was withdrawn. Within a few years the warriors were returned to the Indian Territory, and in nine years from that time the same Indians were rearmed and remounted, in better condition for war than before, and ripe for an outbreak. The commanding general of the army and the department commander were sent to the Indian Territory, and nearly one-fourth of the army was concentrated in that department to prevent a serious outbreak, endangering the peace of Kansas, Colorado, New Mexico, and Texas, by the same Indians who are now in a threatening condition.

Again, take the Sioux nation, that committed the terrible massacre of '62 in Minnesota, in which it was authoritatively stated that one thousand lives were lost, and a very large military force was employed to bring them under control. Thirty of the principal leaders were tried and hanged, but yet that experience did not deter others of the same Indians from engaging in the subsequent wars of the Sioux nation. In 1867 the Sioux were again in a condition of hostility, and the Fetterman massacre occurred, the

Indians being led by the same man, (Red Cloud) who is said recently to have been instrumental in causing dissatisfaction among the different tribes. Treaties were made with them in 1869, but in 1876, they were again openly hostile, spreading terror over a vast section of the country, embracing a portion of the two Dakotas, Montana, Northern Nebraska, and a part of Wyoming. The massacre on the Little Big Horn followed in 1876, in which two hundred and sixty officers and soldiers under General Custer perished. After two seasons of campaigning against them by the United States troops, during the winter of 1875 and the summer of 1876, and the terribly severe winter campaign of 1876 and 1877, upwards of five thousand agreed to surrender, and nine of their principal men gave themselves as hostages that the tribes would surrender on the Yellowstone or at the different agencies; which they did with the exception of two bands under the leadership of Lame Deer and Sitting Bull. The former was killed in the following May, and the latter driven to Canada and kept north of the boundary for three years, until he and his followers finally surrendered between 1877 and 1881.

For four years from 1877 to 1881 they were under military control, and many of them were made self-sustaining. They were disarmed and dismounted, their war ponies were sold and the proceeds returned to them in domestic stock, and in a few years they had a large herd of cattle, and wagons and cultivated fields. In 1881 they were ordered to be sent down the Yellowstone and Missouri to the southern agencies, and although they implored the different officers to write or telegraph to the authorities in Washington to leave them where their crops were developing in the fields, they were loaded on five large steamboats and shipped down the river, and turned over to the Indian agent at Standing Rock Agency.

Many of these same Indians are now in a condition of threatening hostility. Within the short space of ten years we find the condition of the Cheyennes and Sioux Indians to be as follows; the fine herd of cattle belonging to the Cheyennes has disappeared. They claim that it has been partly taken by the whites, and that they were obliged to use the remainder for food. They claim that it was almost impossible for them to obtain food without committing depredations, and they stated in the presence of a commission recently visiting them that they were "compelled to eat their dogs in order to sustain life." The fact that they have not received sufficient food is admitted by the agents and the officers of the government who have had opportunities of knowing, and their condition is again as threatening as at any time when they have not been in hostility.

The Sioux Indians during that time were under the charge of civil agents, who have been frequently changed, and often inexperienced. Many of the tribes have become rearmed and remounted, and have assumed a threatening attitude. They claim that the government has not fulfilled its treaties and has failed to make large enough appropriations for their support; they also claim that they have suffered for the want of food, and the evidence of this is beyond question and sufficient to satisfy any unprejudiced, intelligent mind. The statements of the officers, inspectors both of the Military and the Interior Department, of agents, of missionaries and civilians familiar with their condition, leave no room for reasonable doubt that this is one of the principal causes of the present disturbance. While statements may be made as to the amount of money that has been expended by the Government to feed the different tribes, and while there is no intention of questioning the honesty of all concerned, the manner of distributing those appropriations will furnish one reason for the deficit.

Another cause is the unfortunate failure of the crops in the plains country during the last two years. It has been almost impossible for the Indians to raise anything from the ground for self-support; in fact, white settlers have been very unfortunate and their losses have been serious and universal through a large section of that country. They have struggled on from year to year; occasionally they would raise good crops of corn, which they were compelled to sell for from fourteen to twenty cents per bushel, while in the season of drought their labor was almost entirely lost. So serious have been their misfortunes that many hundreds have left the country within the last few years, passing over the mountains to the Pacific slope or returning to the east banks of the Missouri and Mississippi.

The Indian, however, cannot migrate from one part of the United States to another; neither can he obtain employment as readily as white people, either upon or beyond the Indian reservations. He must remain in comparative idleness and accept the results of the drought. This creates a feeling of discontent, even among the loyal and well-disposed, while there is quite a large element that is hostile and opposed to every process of civilization.

In this condition of affairs the Indians realize the inevitable, and as they see their numbers gradually diminishing, their strength and power gone, they pray to their God for some supernatural help to aid them in the restoration of their former independence, and for the destruction of their enemies. At this stage emissaries from a certain religious sect or people living on the western slope of the Rocky Mountains came among them announcing that the real Messiah had appeared; and in order to convince themselves, delegations of Sioux, Cheyennes, and other tribes left their reservations a year ago last November, travelling through the Arrapahoe and Shoshone reservations in Wyoming, and thence via the Union Pacific they passed into Utah, and were joined by others, Bannocks and Pi-Utes, until they came to a large conclave of whites and Indians in Nevada. They were there told that those present were all believers in this new religion, that they were all an oppressed people, that the whites and Indians there were all the same, and that the Messiah had returned to them.

So well was this deception played by men masquerading and personating Christ, that they made these superstitious savages believe that all who had faith in this "new religion" would occupy tne earth, and all who do not would be destroyed; and they were told that which is most precious to the Indian heart, that the spirits of their departed relatives would be resurrected, and that after the whites were destroyed they would come back driving vast herds of buffaloes and wild horses. They there met the representatives of fourteen tribes of Indians, and after several months they returned to the various tribes and announced what they had seen and heard, fully convinced that what had been told them was true. But in order to gratify the savage nature of the warlike Sioux they agreed that *acts* would be necessary to appease or hasten the coming of the Messiah; that they must help remove the whites and thereby show their faith by their works.

To the disaffected, turbulent, hostile spirit of such men as Sitting Bull and others this was like a revelation; nothing could be more gratifying; and the false prophets and medicine-men immediately took advantage of the condition of the Indians to proclaim this doctrine and spread disaffection among the different tribes.

In early life Sitting Bull gained his reputation as a warrior by incessantly organizing and leadding raiding parties and by his perpetual hostility to the white race. Few Indians have appeared on this continent who have been more successful in organizing and drawing to them large bodies of the discontented of their people. Emissaries travelled in various directions, not alone from his tribe but more especially from the Shoshones and Arrapahoes, who have been to some extent peaceable for many years, going to the different tribes and endeavoring to persuade them to this belief. Emissaries from Sitting Bull carried the tidings to the different tribes to get all the arms and ammunition possible, and meet all the warriors near the Black Hills in the spring. They visited the band of Sioux Indians north of the British boundary, and sympathy and promise of support were returned. The first sign of disturbance was to be the signal for the gathering of the warriors.

During the last few years, and while there was apparently no danger of immediate outbreak, the Indians have been getting a large amount of ammunition and arms. The Indian's instinct is always to obtain some weapon of warfare or defence, and if he cannot obtain a rifle, he will get a knife or a bow and arrow. His favorite weapon, and one he has been most desirous of obtaining, is the long-range Winchester rifle, which is a rifle of the most effective kind.

The theory that a few lines of railway and the disappearance of the vast herds of buffaloes have made it impracticable for Indians to go to war is erroneous. They are in a better condition for war at present than ever before; they can live upon domestic stock, and there is abundance of it scattered over the plains country and much of the mountain country; and the numerous horse-ranches would furnish them a remount in nearly every valley. The Nez Perces, Bannocks, and Apaches in their recent wars lived and moved entirely upon the stock of white settlers. The area over which they could roam is the country west of the Missouri River between the Canadian boundary and the Rio Grande. It contains a very sparse population that has been struggling to plant homes.

Another reason of encouragement to the Indians to assume hostilities, and one of which their false prophets take advantage in influencing their followers, is the misfortunes that have occured to the white people in the plains country during the last few years. Three years ago a very large percentage of the domestic stock was destroyed by the intensely cold winter of 1887, and the losses were ruinous to thousands of white settlers and ranchmen. The drought during the last two years has been very serious, and has caused many of the poor settlers who have been struggling for years to support themselves and their families to leave that country in pursuit of better fields west of the Rocky Mountains or east of the Missouri. This, the false prophets claim, is an indication that the Great Spirit is angry with the white people for destroying their buffaloes (cattle) and causing them to leave the country, and that in time their buffaloes will return, as well as their dead relatives.

While the Indians have been in this disaffected condition and rearming and remounting, the little army that is the only safeguard between the unprotected settlers and the savage hordes has been employed in other fields, and its supplies and equipments have been seriously curtailed. Congress has fixed the limit of the enlisted men in the army, the number of employees, the number of horses and the number of mules, and the limit is what might be required in time of peace, rather than what is actually required in serious warfare. Congress, however, has not limited Indian wars. This necessarily causes much embarrassment to the United States troops; yet it has been the experience of the army of the United States to cope with the large number of savage tribes, experiencing all the dangers and hardships of a war in which no quarter is expected, and every officer and soldier who enters an Indian campaign realizes that unless he achieves success, naught awaits him but torture or death.

No one who has not experienced it can comprehend or appreciate the fortitude, hardships and sacrifices displayed and endured by our army in its years of experience in Indian warfare; frequently in the wildest and most rugged sections of country, amid canyons, mountains, and lava-beds, under the tropical heats of the south or in the Arctic blizzards of the extreme north; yet, year after year, it discharges whatever service is required of it with most commendable fidelity.

You ask me who is responsible for this condition of affairs. The answer is, both the whites and the Indians.

First—Those white men who have compelled the Indians to live upon limited tracts of land and allowed them to get into the condition in which we now find them, dissatisfied and equipped for war.

Second—Another class of whites are those who have committed the great crime of instilling into the minds of these superstitious and vicious savages the delusion that they have a Messiah among them, and that the white people who do not believe it will be destroyed by some supernatural power: it matters not whether the Indians have been incited by this class of white people in actual words to open hostilities or not; the deceptions that have been practised upon them have aroused their warlike natures until they are in a condition for devastation, plunder, ravage, and all the horrors that savage fiends can inflict upon defenceless and unprotected people.

Third—Another class of people who are responsible are the white men who have made merchandise of the welfare and safety of their own people; in other words, those who have sold thousands of improved magazine long-range rifles and tons of ammunition to savages, which alone enable them to devastate the country. Those Indians could manufacture neither a rifle, a cartridge, nor a knife; yet they are better armed and better supplied with ammunition to-day than at any time in their history.

Fourth—Those who are to blame for this threatened danger are the Indians themselves; and Halleck's description of Red Jacket is not a bad illustration of the Indian's double character. While they have wrongs and grievances that have been fully enumerated, at the same time they have friends anxious to protect their interests; but, notwithstanding this, they would in justification of some real or imaginary wrong, or prompted by some wild, savage religious frenzy, ravage a country and brain the innocent prattling babe with fiendish delight as readily as they would meet a stalwart foe.

If you ask for a remedy that will prevent the possibility of such a condition of affairs in the future, I would say that I have not changed the opinion formed and stated thirteen years ago. After careful observation of all the principal tribes in the United States, I believe that those people who have been, and are still, a terror to the peace and good order of certain States and Territories should be placed under some government just and strong enough to control them.

The time has arrived when the lifes, welfare, prosperity, and future of those great States are too precious and too valuable to be jeopardized by these yearly alarms and frequent Indian wars. While thousands of people have fled from their little homes, and abandoned most of their property, to seek shelter and refuge in any place where it could be obtained, and while thousands of resolute and intrepid officers and soldiers are enduring the severity of a Dakota winter to hold in restraint these tribes of turbulant savages, it is hoped that some conclusion will be reached by the Government to permanently end the present state of affairs. The subject is too serious for selfishness, acrimony, or partianship. It requires judicious, humane, and patriotic treatment.

As a sample of the difficulties General Miles had to contend with in drawing his cordon around the hostiles and gradually forcing a surrender against which they could hardly murmur, we instance the murder of Few Tails, who was revered in his tribe, and who ranked as a philosopher among his kind. He was never regarded as other than friendly and his influence was courted whenever negotiations of a serious nature impended. A Pine Ridge correspondent thus tells of his murder, under the date of January 19, 1891:—When treacherous whites in the Bear Butte country wantonly murdered old Few Tails last week, and wounded his squaw, they committed an outrage that has come near ruining General Miles' plans, and stampeding the 5,000 hostiles who are in camp here. Few Tails was a relative of Young-man-afraid-of-his-horses, the only hereditary chief in the Great Sioux nation, and the most powerful leader among his people.

Few Tails' party were on their way to Pine Ridge from a hunt in the Bear Butte country. The party consisted of six bucks, two squaws, twelve ponies and two wagons. They carried with them a pass from General Brooke, and assurances from Captain Taylor that they were peaceable. Not a member of the little band was painted and they carried no ammunition or guns.

Early on the morning of the 11th they started on their journey southward. Before breaking up camp they carefully banked their fires.

They had gone but a short distance when they were fired upon from an ambush by a party of whites. Few Tails fell dead. One bullet pierced his brain and another missile struck him in the breast. His squaw was shot in the leg and breast and probably fatally hurt.

Few Tail's corpse lay among the wild meat in the vehicle, while his squaw managed to crawl to the bushes, where she hid for a day before setting out on her painful tramp to Pine Ridge, one hundred miles away. The rest of the Indians abandoned the other wagon and fled, and she supposed that they too, were slain. About twenty yards from the place where Few Tails was killed, Lieutenant Marshall, of the Eighth Cavalry, found twenty or more Winchester rifle cartridges in a clump of bushes where the murderers were in hiding when the Indians were passing along. On the day of the murder two young men by the name of Culbertson called at the camp of Colonel Merriam, of the Seventh Infantry, and admitted that they had killed the Indians, but claimed that the band had been caught stealing horses. Colonel Merriam, in his report to General Miles, says this story is untrue, and requests that the Governor of South Dakota be advised of the outrage, so that the murderers may be punished. Lieutenant Marshall, in his report, characterizes the killing as cold blooded murder. When the wounded squaw crawled into the camp of the Sixth Cavalry at this place, yesterday, she was almost dead.

So slow had been the transmission of official reports that the wounded woman, although she has stumbled and fallen all the way from Bear Butte, preceded them by a half hour. When she reached the hospital she began to rave about the murder of Few Tails. The Indians who were nursing the other wounded Sioux quickly spread the report that a relative of Young-man-afraid-of-his-horses had been killed by the whites.

Almost instantly there was commotion in the hostile camp. Scouts reported the situation to General Miles, who immediately sent runners after Young-man-afraid-of-his-horses. When the chief appeared at headquarters and learned of the ingratitude of the whites he scowled, and for a few moments refused to be pacified. Meantime the hostiles were saddling up their horses on the sides of the buttes and herding their cattle. It is a fact that it took all the diplomacy at the command of General Miles and his staff to win back the good will of the great chief. Finally the latter walked away apparently satisfied that the army at least was not responsible for the assassination, but the fright of the hostiles was intensified to such an extent that the military became alarmed.

Captain Charles King, of the Regular Army, in speaking of the death of Lieutenant Casey, while on a tour of observation and in front of one of the hostile Brule camps, reminds the country of the immense losses of valuable lives occasioned by each Indian uprising. The aggregate is certainly appalling, and to read the list it is fair to conclude that Indian wars, by reason of their frequency, are far more disastrous in the end than a square bout with a foreign nation has ever proved to be. The Captain says:—

"Another brave spirit gone! Another gallant fellow foully and treacherously murdered by the red men, and God alone knows who is to go next."

There was something particularly sad about the killing of Lieutenant Casey. He was one of the pets of the whole service, and by that I mean not the pets described by the Washington correspondents of some of our papers, but a frontier pet—a man loved by his comrades and almost worshipped by his men, because of the genial qualities that seemed to overflow within him.

He was full of wit, fun, and devilment—a ringleader in the pranks of his classmates, and the center of a laughing group at every recreation hour.

He was one of the crack officers of his regiment—Stanley's old Twenty-second.

His selection to organize and command the first troop of Indian scouts raised for service in the North-west was an admirable one. Heart and soul he threw himself into the task, and his enthusiasm had even reached and impressed the Secretary of War.

Mr. Remington, the artist, who has done such yeoman service in bringing our frontier life and service before the eyes of the people, was with him at the moment of his tragic end, and has told in simple but thrilling words the story of how the Brules first invited his coming, then turned him back, and, like the brutal cowards they are, shot him dead the instant his head was turned.

Where will it end?

Only a fortnight ago we got the news of Wallace's death at Wounded Knee, and of the wounding of Garlington, Mann and Hawthorne. Does anyone realize, I wonder, what losses the little army has sustained in our battling with the hostiles, for whom, if the truth were told, we feel far more sympathy and friendship as a rule than do the people at large? It would be far too long a story to tell of the years spent in close proximity to the various tribes, the intimate knowledge acquired of their actual needs, their real wrongs, their fancied grievances, their usual treatment at the hands of the politically appointed Indian agents.

Just at this moment I am mainly impressed with the truth and far reaching extent of the conviction forced upon me years ago—that the army is but the buffer interposed between the white and the red man, and no matter whether the original wrong is wrought by agent or Indian, when the latter takes the warpath it is the soldier who suffers.

I am bound to say that once he digs up the hatchet and prepares for business our noble red man forgets the favors and hospitalities shown him perhaps for years by his soldier friends, and he eagerly draws a bead on Captain this or Lieutenant that, around whose doorsteps he has been begging or in whose kitchen he has been fed more times than he can count on his cartridges, and he is sure to have a plentiful supply of these. He buys them between times as he does his Winchester or Henry at ten times their cost price in furs or peltries from the very settlers who are the first to importune the Government for troops and arms as soon as trouble comes.

If Indian war is not rough on officers then statistics are forked-tongued, as the Indian would say, but I hope no life insurance agency will believe them. But let us look at the list of officers slain by our red men in these days of piping peace. It is formidable.

Brigadier General E. R. S. Canby, massacred at the Modoc Council in the Lava Beds, April 1873—a damnable piece of treachery, as was the almost simultaneous murder of Lieutenant Will Sherwood, Twenty-First Infantry, whom they enticed to meet them by waving a flag of truce and then shot him down when he came to them "with peace in his outspread hands."

Lieutenant Colonel William H. Lewis, Nineteenth Infanty, in Western Kansas, September 1878.

Lieutenant Colonel George A. Custer, Seventh Cavalry, at the battle of Little Big Horn, in Montana, June 25, 1876.

Major Joel H. Elliott, Seventh Cavalry, at the battle of the Washita, Indian Territory, November 19, 1868.

Surgeon Benjamin Tappan, Arizona, March, 1866.

SENTIMENT RESPECTING THE UPRISING. 313

Captain Fred H. Brown, Eighteenth Infantry, near Fort Phil. Kearney, Wyoming Territory, and Captain W. J. Fetterman, Twenty-seventh Infantry, and Lieutenant George W. Grummond, Eighteenth Infantry, in the same desperate battle with Red Cloud's surrounding warriors. December 21, 1866.

Lieutenant H. S. Bingham, Second Cavalry, near the same spot and by the same Indians, December 6, only two weeks before.

Lieutenant Lyman S. Kidder, Second Cavalry, near Fort Wallace, Kansas, July, 1867.

Lieutenant John C. Jennes, Twenty-seventh Infantry, near Fort Phil Kearney, August, 1867. (A fatal neighborhood this, both then and thereafter).

Lieutenant John Madigan, First Cavalry, Pitt River, California, September, 1867.

Lieutenant Sigismund Sternberg, Twenty-seventh Infantry, Fort C. F. Smith (near Fort Phil. Kearney), August 1, 1867.

Captain Louis M. Hamilton, Seventh Cavalry, leading the charge on Black Kettle's village, on the Washita, November 27, 1868. (Same battle in which Major Elliott was killed).

Lieutenant Frederick H. Beecher, Third Infantry, September 17, 1868, Arickaree Fork of the Republican, Western Kansas. (Colonel

George A. Forsyth, of Sheridan's staff, wounded and crippled for life in the same fight).

Lieutenant **William Russell, Jr.,** Fourth Cavalry, near Lampasas, Texas, May 15, 1870.

Lieutenant C. B. Stambaugh, Second Cavalry, near Miner's Delight, Wyoming, May, 1870.

* Lieutenant Howard B. Cushing, Third Cavalry (brother of Albemarle Cushing, of the Navy), Arizona, May 5, 1870.

Captain Franklin **Yeaton,** Third Cavalry, (died of wounds received in same fight).

Lieutenant Fred. R. Vincent, Ninth Cavalry, fight at Howard's Wells, Texas, April 20, 1872.

Lieutenant Eben Crosby, Seventeenth Infantry, on survey of Northern Pacific Railroad, October 5, 1872.

Lieutenant **Lewis** Adair, Twenty-second Infantry, same fight.

Lieutenant Reid T. Stewart, Fifth Cavalry, Arizona, August 27, 1872, (murdered by Apaches).

Captain Evan Thomas, Fourth Artillery, Lava Beds, California, April 26, 1873, battle with Modocs.

Lieutenant **Albion Howe,** Fourth Artillery, same fight

Lieutenant Arthur Cranston, Fourth Artillery, same fight.

Captain Fred H. Brown, Eighteenth Infantry, near Fort Phil. Kearney, Wyoming Territory, and Captain W. J. Fetterman, Twenty-seventh Infantry, and Lieutenant George W. Grummond, Eighteenth Infantry, in the same desperate battle with Red Cloud's surrounding warriors. December 21, 1866.

Lieutenant H. S. Bingham, Second Cavalry, near the same spot and by the same Indians, December 6, only two weeks before.

Lieutenant Lyman S. Kidder, Second Cavalry, near Fort Wallace, Kansas, July, 1867.

Lieutenant John C. Jennes, Twenty-seventh Infantry, near Fort Phil Kearney, August, 1867. (A fatal neighborhood this, both then and thereafter).

Lieutenant John Madigan, First Cavalry, Pitt River, California, September, 1867.

Lieutenant Sigismund Sternberg, Twenty-seventh Infantry, Fort C. F. Smith (near Fort Phil. Kearney), August 1, 1867.

Captain Louis M. Hamilton, Seventh Cavalry, leading the charge on Black Kettle's village, on the Washita, November 27, 1868. (Same battle in which Major Elliott was killed).

Lieutenant Frederick H. Beecher, Third Infantry, September 17, 1868, Arickaree Fork of the Republican, Western Kansas. (Colonel

George A. Forsyth, of Sheridan's staff, wounded and crippled for life in the same fight).

Lieutenant William Russell, Jr., Fourth Cavalry, near Lampasas, Texas, May 15, 1870.

Lieutenant C. B. Stambaugh, Second Cavalry, near Miner's Delight, Wyoming, May, 1870.

Lieutenant Howard B. Cushing, Third Cavalry (brother of Albemarle Cushing, of the Navy), Arizona, May 5, 1870.

Captain Franklin Yeaton, Third Cavalry, (died of wounds received in same fight).

Lieutenant Fred. R. Vincent, Ninth Cavalry, fight at Howard's Wells, Texas, April 20, 1872.

Lieutenant Eben Crosby, Seventeenth Infantry, on survey of Northern Pacific Railroad, October 5, 1872.

Lieutenant Lewis Adair, Twenty-second Infantry, same fight.

Lieutenant Reid T. Stewart, Fifth Cavalry, Arizona, August 27, 1872, (murdered by Apaches).

Captain Evan Thomas, Fourth Artillery, Lava Beds, California, April 26, 1873, battle with Modocs.

Lieutenant Albion Howe, Fourth Artillery, same fight.

Lieutenant Arthur Cranston, Fourth Artillery, same fight.

Lieutenant George M. Harris, Fourth Artillery, died of wounds received in same fight.

Lieutenant T. F. Wright, Twelfth Infantry, same fight.

Lieutenant Jacob Almy, Fifth Cavalry, killed while protecting an Indian agent, San Carlos, A. T., May 27, 1873.

The above have laid down their lives in what may be called open warfare, but think of the long list of those who have been slain by treachery—who went down in cold blood at the hands of assassins. The sad list foots up as follows:—

Lieutenant William L. Sherwood, Twenty-first Infantry, killed by Modocs, who enticed him to them by waving a flag of truce, April 11, 1873.

Lieutenant L. H. Robinson, Fourteenth Infantry, murdered by Sioux, Cottonwood Creek, Wyoming, February 9, 1874.

Captain Myles W. Keogh, Seventh Cavalry, battle of the Little Horn, Montana, June 25, 1876.

Captain George W. Yates, Seventh Cavalry, same fight.

Captain T. W. Custer, Seventh Cavalry, same fight.

Lieutenant and Adjutant W. W. Cooke, Seventh Cavalry, same fight.

Assistant Surgeon George E. Lord, U. S. A., same fight.

Lieutenant A. E. Smith, Seventh Cavalry, same fight.

Lieutenant Donald McIntosh, Seventh Cavalry (Reno's battalion), **same date.**

Lieutenant James Calhoun, Seventh Cavalry, same fight.

Lieutenant James E. Porter, Seventh Cavalry, same fight.

Lieutenant Benjamin W. Hodgson, Seventh Cavalry (Reno's battalion), **same date.**

Lieutenant James G. Sturgis, Seventh Cavalry, same fight.

Lieutenant W. Van W. Reilly, Seventh Cavalry, same fight.

Lieutenant John J. Crittenden, Twenty-second Infantry, **same fight.**

Lieutenant H. M. Harrington, Seventh Cavalry, same fight.

Lieutenant John A. McKinney, Fourth Cavalry, Powder River, Wyoming, November 25, 1876.

Captain Owen Hale, Seventh Cavalry, Bear's Paw battle ground, **leading the charge on Chief Joseph's band, September, 30, 1877.**

Lieutenant J. Williams Biddle, Seventh Cavalry, **fell beside** his captain in same charge.

Captain William Logan, Seventh Infantry, **battle of Big** Hole Pass, Montana, August 9, 1877.

Lieutenant James H. Bradley, Seventh Infantry (the same officer who made the daring night ride the previous year to locate the survivors of the battle on the Little Horn) killed in the same fight.

Lieutenant William L. English, Seventh Infantry, same fight.

Lieutenant E. R. Heller, Twenty-first Infantry, White Bird Creek, Idaho, June 17, 1877.

Captain E. C. Hentig, Sixth Cavalry, Arizona, August 30, 1881.

Lieutenant George W. Smith, Ninth Cavalry, New Mexico, August 19, 1881.

Lieutenant Seward Mott, Tenth Cavalry, Arizona, March 11, 1887.

Lieutenant Sevier M. Raines, First Cavalry, Craig's Mountain, Idaho, July 3, 1877.

Captain Andrew S. Bennett, Fifth Infantry, Clark's Fork Mountain, Wyoming, September 4, 1878.

Major Thomas T. Thornburgh, Fourth Infantry, Milk River, Colorado, September 29, 1879.

Lieutenant William B. Weir, Ordnance Deparment, killed by Utes, White River, Colorado, October 20, 1879.

Add to these the names of the gifted and popular Dr. Maddox and Lieutenant J. Hansell French, Tenth Cavalry, who were killed in the later Apache campaign, and of gallant Captain Wallace, Seventh Cavalry, (the fourth captain to be killed fighting at the head of "K" troop), and now of "Ned" Casey, of the Twenty-second Infantry, and augment that by the list four times its size, of the officers now maimed and crippled by the wounds received in this savage and inglorious warfare, and it must be admitted that the percentage of casualties is indeed heavy. And then think of the enlisted men!

We appropriate anywhere from five to ten millions of dollars per annum to the Indians and to their affairs, and if the same amount of money should be devoted to any class of white people, benefaction would be regarded as one of the most liberal public charities in the known world. It is a very difficult thing, as every practical philanthropist knows, to make gifts with such wise discretion as not to do more harm than good; and it is quite possible that the red men would be as well off in the long run if the Government should stop trying to devote to their welfare an average of, say, seven millions a year, and, after decent notice, should cut them square off and not give them another cent in the way of alms. If we should leave them to shift for themselves, as Canada does; let them get along how they can, get rich if they can—starve if they must—they would not bring more reproach and disgrace on the country than they now do. It is reasonably certain, however, that we shall never come to such a conclusion. We can let our own flesh and blood take the chances of good or evil fortune without a shadow of thought or care, and if a white man perishes in misery inconceivable and all his tribe with him, the collective conscience feels no twinge, and nobody but the cranks, communists, and backward-looking social reformers ever dreams of taking any Government action to prevent or remedy such dire disasters, so long as it is our own people who suffer and are crushed to death in the struggle for existence. But with Lo the poor Indian the case is different. He must have a better show than we even pretend to give our own, and the community feels a tender sense of responsibility for his welfare that is hurt and outraged whenever our clumsy attempts to help him are found to miscarry, as charitable undertakings so commonly do.

We have taken the lands of these natives, occupied their hunting grounds, and deprived them of the means of continuing their savage existence; and now we, the people, in our national capacity, feel that we must do what we can to make their condition tolerable, and aid them to live in some other than the savage state we have compelled them to abandon. It is for that reason and for that purpose we are willing to set aside every year such vast sums for their use and behoof.

We should, however, learn a little by experience. We know only too well, and all the world knows, how, a great deal of waste and harm is brought about, and it will be to our shame and discredit if we do not seek to profit by that knowledge. We have seen our money squandered and the Indians driven to desperation by deception and fraud, because we have allowed the national bounty to become the prey of liars and thieves. That should never be again. Not one dollar should be appropriated by Congress for the alleged benefit of the Indians which will go, as we do know it will go under the present agency system, into the pockets of plunderers.

www.ingramcontent.com/pod-product-compliance
Lightning Source LLC
Chambersburg PA
CBHW020321240426
43673CB00039B/881